T0363860

# Eyes Open 4

### WORKBOOK
### with Digital Pack

## Vicki Anderson with Eoin Higgins

CAMBRIDGE
UNIVERSITY PRESS

Discovery
EDUCATION

# Contents

# Starter Unit

## Past simple vs. past continuous

**1** ★★ **Complete the text with the past simple or past continuous form of the verbs in the box.**

> not look   decide   concentrate   still hold
> tell   fall   arrive   pull   call   walk (x2)
> try   notice   see

A young man ¹___was walking___ along the side of the river near his home when he ²_____ to check his Facebook page. Because he ³_____ on his phone, he ⁴_____ where he was going and ⁵_____ into the river. Luckily, a couple who ⁶_____ on the other side of the river ⁷_____ what happened, and ⁸_____ the emergency services. When the rescuers ⁹_____ to save him, the man ¹⁰_____ to get out of the water. He ¹¹_____ them that he couldn't swim. While the rescuers ¹²_____ him out of the water, one of them ¹³_____ that he ¹⁴_____ his mobile phone!

## Question words

**2** ★★ **Complete the questions with the words in the box. Then match the questions (1–7) with the answers (a–g).**

> Why   How   When   Who   Which   ~~Where~~   What

1   ___Where___ shall we go to have lunch?   _e_
2   _____ shop shall we go in next?   ___
3   _____ didn't you go on the trip to the castle?   ___
4   _____ did you go to the cinema with?   ___
5   _____ did the magician do that trick?   ___
6   _____ does the library close?   ___
7   _____ did you enjoy the most?   ___

a   I went there last year.
b   My sister and my cousins.
c   Nine o'clock, I think.
d   I loved the karaoke.
e   There's a picnic place over there.
f   I want to go in the shoe shop.
g   No idea, but it was amazing!

## -ed and -ing adjectives

**3** ★ **Circle the correct words.**
1   She was so **interested** / interesting in her Facebook posts that she missed her bus stop.
2   Why wasn't she more **worried / worrying** about failing the exam?
3   I think speaking in public is a **terrified / terrifying** experience, but she's always really calm.
4   I didn't think the museum was **bored / boring**! I learned a lot.
5   The boy who rescued the dog had an **excited / exciting** story to tell his friends.
6   They all felt very **tired / tiring** after the walk.

# Starter Unit

## Phrasal verbs

**4** ★ **Rewrite the parts of the sentences in *italics* using the phrasal verbs in the box.**

> come back  ~~pick up~~  find out
> set off  chill out  look round

1 I can *come and get you* at your
house if you like.        *pick you up*

2 It's a big zoo. We need hours to *go
and see* every section.        _____

3 All our exams are finished, so we
can just *relax* this weekend.        _____

4 Did you *discover* what time the
concert starts tomorrow?        _____

5 We *started the journey* at six o'clock
in the morning.        _____

6 If you don't like working in New York,
you can *return* to your job here.        _____

## Energy issues

**5** ★ **Find five more verbs for energy issues in the wordsquare. Two of them have prepositions.**

| w | a | s | t | e | s | k | l |
|---|---|---|---|---|---|---|---|
| o | v | a | z | a | w | o | e |
| b | i | v | c | r | i | p | a |
| a | r | e | d | s | t | u | v |
| n | e | j | l | h | c | o | e |
| d | d | r | q | u | h | m | a |
| t | u | r | n | d | o | w | n |
| o | c | t | a | p | f | u | n |
| n | e | x | t | h | f | f | o |

**6** ★ **Complete the sentences with the correct form of the verbs in Exercise 5.**

1 If we want to ____*save*____ our planet, we need
to use less energy every day.

2 My little brother never _____ the TV when
he stops watching it. Why is he so lazy?

3 Can we _____ the air conditioning, please?
It's too cold in here!

4 We have managed to _____ how much
electricity we use. Now we use 35% less.

5 Paul, you _____ your computer on again
when you went out! It's been on all day!

6 We try not to _____ water in our house.
We all have short showers, not baths.

## Present perfect and past simple

**7** ★★ **Complete the email with the present perfect or past simple form of the verbs in brackets.**

> ✉ *Your*MAIL   ⊕ New   Reply | ▼   Delete   Junk | ▼
>
> Hi Leona,
> How's life back home? We ¹___*have been*___
> (be) on holiday in Amsterdam all week!
> We ²_____ (set off) for the
> airport on Sunday morning, but the plane
> ³_____ (not take off) until the
> evening because there ⁴_____
> (be) a problem with the engine. Finally, we
> ⁵_____ (arrive) at the apartment
> at midnight. ☹
> ⁶_____ (you/go) to Amsterdam?
> It's an amazing city. Up to now, we
> ⁷_____ (spend) lots of time just
> looking round the city centre at all the old
> houses and canals. Of course, in the last
> few days my parents ⁸_____
> (make) lots of plans for our stay, but now my
> brother ⁹_____ (decide) he just
> wants to chill out before he starts university!
> So yesterday, I ¹⁰_____ (go) on
> a trip to see some windmills with my parents
> and he ¹¹_____ (stay) in the
> apartment. Today we ¹²_____
> (book) online tickets for the Van Gogh
> museum, though, and he is coming with us.
> Will write again soon,
> Carrie

## *make* and *do*

**8** ★ **Complete the sentences with *make* or *do*.**

1 Be careful or you'll ____*make*____ a mistake.

2 Sssssh! Please don't _____ a noise.

3 Did you _____ anything interesting today?

4 We mustn't _____ a mess.

5 We need to _____ the right thing.

6 I can't _____ a phone call here.

7 It's difficult for some people to _____
friends.

8 Did you _____ all your homework last
night?

# Starter Unit

## Present perfect with *still*, *yet*, *already* and *just*

**9** ★ **Complete the sentences with *still*, *yet*, *already* or *just*.**

1 Look, I've ____*just*____ bought some new football boots. What do you think?

2 **Dad:** Have you switched off your computer _____ ? We're leaving now.
**Ollie:** Don't worry, Dad! I've _____ done it. I did it ages ago!

3 Have you bought Kerry a birthday present _____ ?

4 I've _____ packed most of the things we need for the trip, but I haven't found my passport _____ . Have you seen it?

5 **Anna:** Jacinta dropped her bracelet in the garden. She _____ hasn't found it.
**Jacinta:** *[in the garden]* Hurray!
**Sue:** It sounds like she's _____ found it. Thank goodness for that!

## Art around us

**10** ★ **Match the words in the box with the definitions. There are two extra words.**

> microphone ~~mural~~ orchestra portrait exhibition gallery juggler sculpture

1 a painting on a wall ____*mural*____

2 a place you can see paintings or other art _____

3 a 3D work of art made from stone, metal or other materials _____

4 a group of works of art all together, you can see this in 2 above _____

5 a gadget you sing or play into to make the sound louder _____

6 a painting of a person _____

## Word order in questions

**11** ★ **Put the words in order to make questions.**

1 holiday / going / Who / are / with / you / on / ?
*Who are you going on holiday with?*

2 does / the / When / start / safari / ?
_____

3 see / can / we / there / animals / What / ?
_____

4 flight / airport / go / does / Which / from / the / ?
_____

5 did / park / How / get / to / she / safari / the / ?
_____

6 any / you / lions / yet / seen / Have / ?
_____

## Subject/object questions

**12** ★ **Circle the correct words in the table.**

| | |
|---|---|
| 1 | In the sentence 'I saw Luis.', Luis is the **subject / object**. |
| 2 | In the sentence 'Luis saw me.', Luis is the **subject / object**. |
| 3 | In the question 'Who did you see?', 'Who' is the **subject / object**. The answer is: **'I saw Luis.' / 'Luis saw me.'** |
| 4 | In the question 'Who saw you?', 'Who' is the **subject / object**. The answer is: **'I saw Luis.' / 'Luis saw me.'** |

**13** ★★ **Complete the conversation with the past simple form of the verbs in brackets. Use auxiliary verbs and pronouns where necessary.**

**Sam:** Hi Joe! When [1] ____*did you get*____ (get) back?

**Joe:** Yesterday afternoon.

**Sam:** Who [2] _____ (go) on the school exchange?

**Joe:** Everyone in my class.

**Sam:** What [3] _____ (happen) when you arrived?

**Joe:** We went to meet our families.

**Sam:** Who [4] _____ (stay) with?

**Joe:** I stayed with a boy called Jean.

**Sam:** What kind of food [5] _____ (eat)?

**Joe:** Lots of home cooking – Jean's dad's a great cook.

**Sam:** What [6] _____ (do) there?

**Joe:** We went on trips and had lessons.

**Sam:** What trip [7] _____ (like) best?

**Joe:** The riverboat trip.

**Sam:** Who [8] _____ (speak) the best French now?

**Joe:** Well, I don't know. I learned a lot so maybe it's me!

# Starter Unit

## Adventure sports and activities

**14** ★ Use the clues to complete the crossword.

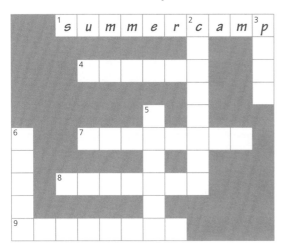

**Across**

1  Young people often go to this in July or August. (2 words)
4  Going on this is a good way to see wild animals.
7  You do this type of long walk in the mountains.
8  You need a boat and a good wind for this activity.
9  You do this kind of visit with another school.

**Down**

2  You do this in the mountains, or inside on a wall.
3  See 6 down.
5  You do this in snow, normally in the winter.
**6 and 3 down**  A fun place with lots of rides and shows. (2 words)

## Present perfect with *ever, never, for* and *since*

**15** ★ Complete the sentences with *ever, never, for* or *since*.

1  We've lived in this flat _____*for*_____ eight years.
2  I've _____ been to summer camp, but I'd like to go one day.
3  She's studied ballet _____ 2009.
4  Have you _____ seen a shooting star?
5  That film's been on at the cinema _____ weeks. It's really popular.
6  We've been best friends _____ we started primary school.
7  They've _____ come to visit us here. We always go there.
8  Has he _____ met any famous actors?

## Present perfect questions

**16** ★★ Write present perfect questions for these answers.

1  *How long have you had your phone?*
   I've had my phone for a year.
2  _____
   No, I've never met a famous person.
3  _____
   We've lived in this flat since I was a baby.
4  _____
   Yes, I visited this gallery last year with my mum.
5  _____
   No, she hasn't been here for a long time.
6  _____
   He started playing the guitar when he was twelve.

## Survival essentials

**17** ★ Complete the words.

1  s*un*_____
   c*ream*_____

2  p_____-
   k_____

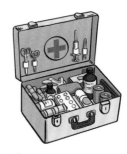

3  s_____
   b_____

4  f_____
   a_____
   k_____

5  c_____
   l_____

6  w_____
   b_____

# 1 Trends

## Vocabulary

### Clothes

**1** ★ Write the words for the clothes.

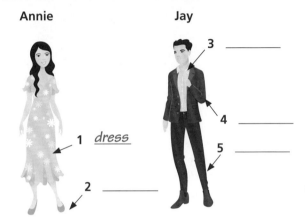

Annie

Jay

1 _dress_

2 _____

3 _____

4 _____

5 _____

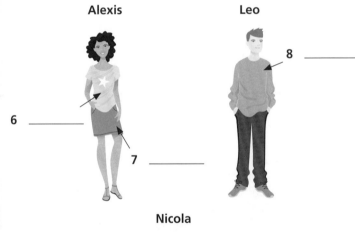

Alexis

Leo

6 _____

7 _____

8 _____

Nicola

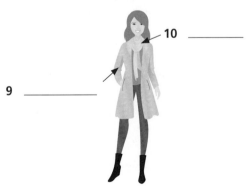

9 _____

10 _____

**2** ★ Put the letters in order to make ten words to describe clothes.

1 tfal      _flat_
2 tpisyr    _____
3 dteift    _____
4 aeehlrt   _____
5 gygab     _____

6 ikls      _____
7 oloc      _____
8 wylfreo   _____
9 nedmi     _____
10 ghitt    _____

**3** ★★ Look at the pictures in Exercise 1 again. Complete the descriptions with words from Exercise 2 and the people's names.

1 _____Jay_____'s wearing a ___leather___ jacket, a _____ shirt and _____ jeans.
2 _____'s wearing a _____ dress and _____ shoes.
3 _____'s wearing a _____ jumper.
4 _____'s wearing a _____ coat and a _____ scarf.
5 _____'s wearing a _____ skirt and a _____ T-shirt.

**4** ★★ Complete the conversation with words from Exercises 1 and 2.

**Nic:** Hi Zac, have you been shopping?
**Zac:** Yes. Tell me what you think. Look at this denim [1]___jacket___ . It's the latest fashion. I got a bigger size because I like [2]_____ clothes, not fitted ones.
**Nic:** It's really cool! What else?
**Zac:** I got two warm wool [3]_____ for the winter. This plain blue one, and this [4]_____ one, I really like the red and green together.
**Nic:** Wow! It's very bright!
**Zac:** It's OK, it's not for school! What do you think of these? I needed some new [5]_____ as my feet have grown, and these are real [6]_____ , and black. I hope they're comfortable. I prefer trainers but we can't wear them to school. It's crazy!
**Nic:** They look alright. Is that all?
**Zac:** No, I also bought three white [7]_____ for school, totally boring, I hate wearing a uniform and a tie! And finally, a pair of black denim [8]_____ for the weekends, when I don't have to wear trousers.

**5** ★★★ Write about your favourite clothes and what you usually wear. Write at least five sentences. Use vocabulary from Exercises 1 and 2.

*My favourite clothes at the moment are my new tight black jeans and a T-shirt I bought on holiday.*

# Language focus 1

## *used to* and *would*

**1** ★ **Complete the rules in the table.**

| | |
|---|---|
| **1** | We use *used to* and *would* to talk about past _____ . |
| **2** | After both *used to* and *would* we use the _____ form. |
| **3** | We use *did(n't)* in negative and question forms with _____ . |
| **4** | We only use *would* with _____ , like *play* or *go*. We use *used to* with actions and _____ verbs, like *be* or *have*. |

**2** ★ **Complete the sentences with the correct form of *used to* and the verbs in brackets.**

1  In the 1980s, most teenagers
   _____*used to talk*_____ (talk) for hours on the home phone.

2  When you were younger,
   _____ (have) long hair?

3  Every month, she _____ (spend) all her pocket money, but now she saves some.

4  When my granddad went to concerts in the 1960s, people _____ (sit) on the floor!

5  Fifty years ago, young people
   _____ (not listen) to music on the Internet.

6  I think my uncle _____ (be) a New Romantic!

7  Did your parents _____ (like) pop music when they were teenagers?

8  When I was little, my mum
   _____ (buy) all my clothes. I hated them!

**3** ★ **Which five sentences from Exercise 2 can also be written with *would*? Rewrite the sentences here.**

*1 In the 1980s, most teenagers would talk for hours on the home phone.*

_____

_____

_____

_____

_____

_____

_____

**4** ★★ Circle **the correct options. If they are both correct, circle both.**

**A:** What's that photo?

**B:** It's my dad! He ¹used to be / would be in a punk band and they ²used to travel / would travel all over the country to play concerts every weekend. He ³used to have / would have an old van to travel around in.

**A:** ⁴Did your mum use to be / Would your mum be a punk, too?

**B:** Well, sort of. She was a punk rock fan who ⁵used to go / would go to lots of local concerts and she wore punk clothes, but she ⁶didn't use to have / wouldn't have a punk hairstyle because she was still at school and her parents were strict.

**A:** What about your dad's hair?

**B:** Well, look at the photo! His hair's dyed bright green and yellow. Apparently he and his friends ⁷used to do / would do it themselves. Dad met Mum at a concert, but until he changed his hairstyle he ⁸didn't use to go / wouldn't go round to her house because she was worried about what her parents might say!

**A:** I can't believe that's your dad. He ⁹used to look / would look so different! I think I'll go home and ask my parents what they ¹⁰used to look like / would look like when they were teenagers!

**5** ★★★ **Change these sentences so they are true for you.**

1  When I was younger, I would play pirates with my friends in the park.

_____

2  I used to wear make-up at birthday parties.

_____

3  I would choose my own clothes when I was younger.

_____

4  At primary school, we used to do lots of homework.

_____

*We wouldn't play pirates in the park. We would play superheroes or football.*

# Listening and vocabulary

## Listening

**1** ★ 🔊 `01` **Listen to a radio programme about school uniforms. Is the presenter for or against them?**

**2** ★★ 🔊 `01` **Listen again and complete the presenter's notes.**

**Introduction:**
Young people have ¹___**strong**___ feelings about uniforms.
²_____ countries have them,
³_____ countries don't.
In ⁴_____ there was a big discussion about uniforms.

**In favour:**
Pupils feel ⁵_____ of their school; all pupils look the ⁶_____; they can concentrate on
⁷_____, not fashion.

**Against:**
Uniforms are ⁸_____ and uncomfortable;
students ⁹_____ very quickly; teachers can't concentrate on ¹⁰_____;
uniforms aren't ¹¹_____ for some subjects; uniforms don't help
¹²_____ or behaviour.

**Uniforms today:**
Girls can wear ¹³_____; no shirts and ties is ¹⁴_____.

**Discussion:**
You can ¹⁵_____ or email.

## Adjectives and dependent prepositions

**3** ★ **Match the sentence beginnings (1–8) with the sentence endings (a–h).**

1 My sister is so **afraid** ___c___
2 I'm really **disappointed** ___
3 You must be **excited** ___
4 Why are you so **fascinated** ___
5 We're really **happy** ___
6 Is anyone **interested** ___
7 I'm not very **keen** ___
8 She's very **proud** ___

a **with** the clothes we bought yesterday.
b **on** heavy metal, it's too loud.
c **of** insects that she hates going in the garden.
d **of** her dress – she made it herself.
e **in** going to the sales with me on Saturday?
f **by** their new album. It's awful!
g **about** going to the concert next week.
h **by** the lives of celebrities?

**4** ★★ **Complete the text with the adjectives and prepositions from Exercise 3.**

My cousins Andrea and Dani are really different. Dani's ¹___**fascinated by**___ animals and has several pets, including a python. No one in his family is very ²_____ the situation, although he says being ³_____ his snake is silly because it doesn't bite! Andrea's very ⁴_____ music, and she plays the guitar in a new pop band. Their first concert is in ten days and they're really ⁵_____ it, but Andrea is secretly a bit nervous! Dani isn't ⁶_____ music at all – I don't think he ever listens to it – but he's really ⁷_____ his sister's talent, and he wants us all to go to the concert together. I heard the band practising last week and I certainly wasn't ⁸_____ their performance – they're really good!

# Language focus 2

## Past perfect

**1** ★ (Circle) **the correct words in the table.**

| | |
|---|---|
| **1** | We form the past perfect with *have* / *had* and the past participle. |
| **2** | We use the past perfect to talk about an action that happened **before** / **after** another action. |
| **3** | To talk about the most recent of two past actions, we use the **past simple** / **past perfect**. |

**2** ★ **Complete the sentences with the past perfect form of the verbs in brackets.**

1 Before Gianni went to college, he ___had designed___ (design) clothes for his friends.
2 We _____ (not be) at the shops long but we were really bored.
3 _____ (they/change) the uniform before you left school?
4 She _____ (not make) a dress before but it was quite easy.
5 Anna went back when she realised she _____ (leave) her leather jacket at home.
6 When you won the talent show, _____ (you/play) together in any other competitions?

**3** ★★ (Circle) **the correct options in the text.**

When my next-door neighbour Alex ¹(came)/ had come back from his first term at university, he ²changed / had changed completely. He ³grew / had grown his hair long, and, when I saw him, he was wearing baggy cotton clothes instead of the cool clothes he ⁴wore / had worn before. He ⁵looked / had looked like a hippy! When I asked him about his new look, he told me that he ⁶went / had been to a meeting about the environment when he ⁷arrived / had arrived at university, and after a few weeks he ⁸joined / had joined Greenpeace. Now he says he's an eco-activist!

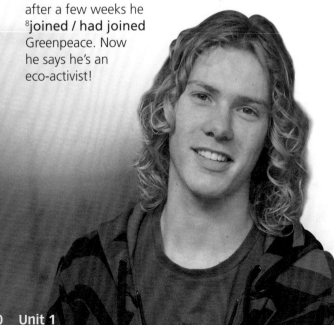

**4** ★★ **Complete the story with the past simple or past perfect form of the verbs in brackets.**

I ¹___saw___ (see) a really nice jumper in town last week, but I ²_____ (not have) enough money with me. So I ³_____ (go) back to the shop on Saturday, but they ⁴_____ (sell) it. I ⁵_____ (feel) really disappointed. But when I ⁶_____ (get) home, my mum ⁷_____ (have) a surprise for me. It ⁸_____ (be) the same jumper! Although I ⁹_____ (not say) anything to her, she ¹⁰_____ (see) it in the shop window and ¹¹_____ (buy) it for me.

**5** ★★★ **Complete the sentences with the past perfect and your own ideas.**

1 My friend finally arrived after _____ _____ .
2 The concert was terrible although we _____ _____ .
3 He was very excited about going to the fashion show because he _____ .
4 She wasn't very good at the new video game because _____ .
5 I didn't go shopping because I _____ _____ .

*My friend finally arrived after I had waited for half an hour.*

## Explore compound nouns

**6** ★★ **Complete the sentences with a word from box A followed by a word from box B.**

Ⓐ | ~~style~~ motor taxi guitar telephone street

Ⓑ | music ~~consultant~~ art box industry driver

1 Famous people often employ a ___style consultant___ to help them decide what clothes to wear.
2 In many big cities today there is a lot of _____ – some of it can be really beautiful, but not always!
3 We went to a concert of classical _____ last night. I wasn't expecting to enjoy it, but it was really relaxing.
4 Everyone in my family works in the _____ – my brother is a mechanic, my dad works in a factory and my mum designs new models.
5 I didn't have my mobile with me yesterday, so I was looking for a _____ , but of course I couldn't find one.
6 I don't think I'd like to work as a _____ because I hate sitting in traffic jams.

# Reading

**1** ★ **Read the article about Comic-Con. Tick (✓) the kind of people who go there.**

famous actors ☐    young people ☐
comic artists ☐    teachers ☐
young children ☐    science-fiction writers ☐

# GEEKS AND SUPERHEROES

Do you like comics? In the 1950s and 60s, many teenagers used to read comics like Batman, Superman or X Men. Some were so fascinated by comics that they would continue reading them when they grew up. They were comic '*geeks*': intelligent, often unsociable young people who identified more with the worlds of fantasy and science fiction than the real world. Geeks still exist today; in the popular TV comedy series *The Big Bang Theory*, the main characters are science geeks who are big fans of comics, fantasy games and Comic-Con.

Comic-Con doesn't try to make money. In fact it describes itself as a **non-profit organisation** that exists to make comics and related art forms more popular through conventions and events. In 1970, a group of about 100 comic fans got together in San Diego, California for the first Comic-Con, or convention. They decided to include not only comics, but also other aspects of popular culture, including fantasy and science-fiction games, books and films from all over the world. Within 30 years, Comic-Con had grown into a huge three-day international convention, with over 120,000 visitors every year. Today there are exhibitions, comics to buy, games to play, educational sessions, talks, a film festival, and even an **awards** ceremony known as the 'Oscars' of the comic industry.

Nowadays, there are comic conventions all over the world, but Comic-Con is the most iconic. It attracts famous film stars, writers and artists from the world of comics. Many of the fans who visit it wear costumes of comic book characters, and sometimes famous stars wear a **disguise** too so they can **wander round** the convention like all the other fans. In 2014, Daniel Radcliffe walked around Comic-Con dressed in a Spiderman costume with a face mask, and no one recognised him. So if you go to Comic-Con, you never know who might be next to you!

**2** ★★ **Complete the sentences with the words in bold from the text.**

1 He's a really good footballer and has won a lot of Player of the Year _____ .

2 My sister and her friends spend all their time on maths problems. They are such _____ !

3 We're going to _____ the old town this morning and look at the little shops.

4 I help at an animal rescue centre. It's a(n) _____ , so they don't pay me.

5 The pop star didn't want anyone to see him, so he went shopping in _____ .

**3** ★★ **Choose the correct answers.**

1 What used to be popular with teenagers in the 1950s and 60s?
   a stories about superheroes
   b science-fiction and fantasy games

2 When was the first Comic-Con convention?
   a in the 1950s    b in 1970

3 What can you see at Comic-Con today?
   a lots of different things
   b comics, games, books and TV comedy programmes

4 How can famous people become 'invisible' at Comic-Con?
   a by behaving like all the other fans
   b by wearing a disguise

**4** ★★ **Read the article again. Who or what is each sentence about?**

1 Teenagers started reading them in the 1950s and 60s.    _comics_

2 They preferred a fantasy world to real life.    _____

3 Its aim is to make the worlds of fantasy and science fiction better known.    _____

4 The 100 people who met in San Diego in 1970 for the first convention.    _____

5 This is what Comic-Con has become.    _____

6 There are more than a hundred thousand of these.    _____

7 You can learn and get information about the world of comics at these.    _____

8 Definitely the most famous comic event internationally.    _____

9 Many of the visitors wear these at Comic-Con.    _____

10 He visited Comic-Con and no one knew who he was.    _____

**5** ★★★ **Do you sometimes read comics? Which ones? Would you like to go to Comic-Con? Why/Why not? Would you wear a costume? Who would you dress as?**

# Writing

## A biography

**1** **Read the biography of The Beach Boys. How long have the band been together?**

The Beach Boys formed in California in 1961. The original members were Brian Wilson, his two brothers, Dennis and Carl, his cousin Mike Love and a friend, Al Jardine. [1]_Although_ the group started around the same time as surfing became much more popular in California, the only member of the band who used to surf was Dennis.

[2]_____ releasing their first album, *Surfin' Safari*, there was a huge rise in the popularity of surf culture on the west coast of the USA. The band had their biggest international hit with their most famous album, *Pet Sounds*, and the single *Good Vibrations*. [3]_____ that time, they were the only American band who could compete with The Beatles and most people think that they are one of America's greatest rock bands.

[4]_____ the years, 36 of their songs have been in the US Top 40 and [5]_____ a result they have sold over 100 million records around the world. Incredibly, the band is still playing – with some different members – and [6]_____ the last few years they have continued to tour.

**2** **Read the biography again. Complete the sentences.**

1 The Beach Boys originally had ____*five*____ members in the band.
2 They started playing music together in _____ , USA.
3 The band were popular at the same time as _____ culture in the USA.
4 Their most successful single was _____ .
5 They've had _____ songs in the Top 40.
6 The band still play together and _____ .

**Useful language** Sequencers and connectors

**3** **Complete the biography with the words in the box.**

> as   After   Over   ~~Although~~   in   During

**4** **Circle the correct words.**

1 After / **In** the last few years, their music has become more popular.
2 **Although / As** they came from the UK, they were also very popular in the USA.
3 They were very famous in the 1990s and **over / during** that time they played a lot of concerts.
4 They formed in 2001 and **in / over** the next 10 years became the biggest band in the world.
5 **Although / After** having three number 1 singles in a row, she began to work with other bands.
6 Jack started a solo career and **as / in** a result the band split up in 2013.

**WRITING TIP**

Make it better! ✓ ✓ ✓
Use *one of* and a superlative adjective to say that what you are talking about is very special in some way.
*The Beatles are **one of the most famous** pop groups ever.*

# Writing

**5** **Complete the sentences with *one of* and the correct form of the adjectives in brackets.**

1 Nirvana were ___one of the most successful___ (successful) bands to come out of Seattle.

2 In the 1990s, U2 were _____ (big) touring bands in the world.

3 Green Day have always been _____ (popular) punk bands in the USA.

4 Beyoncé is _____ (rich) female singers nowadays.

5 For a while, Eminem was _____ (interesting) rap artists in the world.

**6** **Put the words in brackets in the correct place in the sentences.**

1 She had a number 1 hit in 2012 with *Firework*. (again)
   ___She had a number 1 hit again in 2012 with___ ___Firework.___

2 He has sold over 20 million copies of his latest album. (now)
   _____

3 They are touring today after 30 years. (still)
   _____

4 She sang many of her songs in French. (also)
   _____

5 They were one of the most successful bands. (ever)
   _____

> **WRITING TIP**
>
> Make it better! ✓ ✓ ✓
> Talk about the influence or impact the band or artist has had on the present.
> *Elvis Presley died in 1977, but everyone still recognises his music even today.*

**7** **Read the sentences. Which one does not talk about the present?**

1 Their music lives on long after they split up.

2 Her music has become popular with the release of the film.

3 The band's music is still popular today even after 40 years.

4 He was never as successful in his own country as in the USA.

5 She is still touring today and singing the songs everyone loves.

**8** **Read the biography in Exercise 1 again and tick (✓) the information it includes.**

| | |
|---|---|
| information about the members of the band | ✓ |
| their recent work | ☐ |
| the number of number 1 hits | ☐ |
| some of their most famous lyrics | ☐ |
| the number of records they have sold | ☐ |
| problems the band had in their career | ☐ |
| when and where they formed | ☐ |
| the name of a well-known album or single | ☐ |
| the names of bands that they have influenced | ☐ |

## PLAN

**9** **Think of a famous band or artist who started a long time ago but is still successful today. Find out more information about them. Then use the categories in Exercise 8 and make notes.**

## WRITE

**10** **Write a biography of the band or artist. Look at page 17 of the Student's Book to help you.**

_____
_____
_____
_____
_____
_____
_____
_____
_____
_____
_____
_____
_____
_____
_____
_____

## CHECK

**11** **Check your writing. Can you say YES to these questions?**

- Have you used the ideas in Exercise 8?
- Have you used sequencers to order your ideas?
- Have you used connectors to join your ideas?
- Have you used superlatives correctly?
- Have you put the words in the correct order?
- Have you talked about the band or artist's influence or impact on the present?
- Are the spelling and punctuation correct?

**Do you need to write a second draft?**

## Vocabulary
### Clothes

**1** Match the words in the box with the clothes in the pictures. Write the adjectives and the clothes together. There are four extra words.

> denim ~~fitted~~ flat leather silk
> stripy tight flowery baggy cool

1 _a fitted coat_  2 _____

3 _____  4 _____

5 _____  6 _____

☐ Total: 5

## Adjectives and dependent prepositions

**2** Complete the sentences with the correct preposition.

1 Is everyone happy ____with____ spaghetti for supper?
2 My little brother is afraid _____ dogs.
3 She was disappointed _____ her birthday present.
4 My mum says she's proud _____ all her children.
5 He's fascinated _____ insects.
6 Are you excited _____ moving to Australia?
7 I'm not keen _____ the idea of living abroad.
8 I'm not very interested _____ fashion, it's boring.

☐ Total: 7

## Language focus
### *used to* and *would*

**3** Complete the conversation with the correct form of *used to* or *would* and the verbs in brackets. If both are possible, use *would*.

> **A:** My dad $^1$____used to be____ (be) a professional tennis player. He and his coach $^2$_____ (travel) all over the world, and we $^3$_____ (not see) him for weeks or months.
> **B:** $^4$_____ (your mum/be) with you at home?
> **A:** Yes, she $^5$_____ (not like) leaving us, but of course she $^6$_____ (attend) important matches.
> **B:** $^7$_____ (you/go) to any matches?
> **A:** No, not often, because I $^8$_____ (have) school, but in the holidays, yes. Then we $^9$_____ (stay) in big hotels and we $^{10}$_____ (love) it!

☐ Total: 9

## Past perfect

**4** Write sentences with the prompts. Use the past simple and the past perfect in each sentence.

1 The town / change / a lot / when / she / go back / for a visit
_The town had changed a lot when she went back for a visit._

2 I / not see / Melanie / in a dress / before / she / wear / one / to the party
_____

3 After / he / buy / the shoes / he / go / home
_____

4 We / not be / there / long / when / it / start / to rain
_____

5 They / decide / to wait / until / they / finish / their homework
_____

6 the concert / start / when / you / get / there?
_____

☐ Total: 5

## Language builder

**5** (Circle) the correct options.

1 How / (What) was your holiday like?

2 Who **did make / made** this terrible mess? Tidy it up now!

3 He's **just / still** finished practising the guitar, but he **just / still** hasn't done any homework.

4 She's **ever / never** been sailing before.

5 We've lived here **since / for** my sister was born.

6 While they **were trekking / trekked** in the Rockies, he **was falling / fell** and **was breaking / broke** his ankle.

7 I haven't made that phone call **yet / already**. I keep forgetting.

8 When **does start the new school year / does the new school year start**?

9 **Did you use to / Would you** have long hair when you were a teenager, Dad?

10 When we moved to this village, I **lived / had lived** in four different places already.

11 **A: Have you been / Did you go** on a safari before?

   **B:** Yes, I **'ve been / went** on one two years ago. It **'s been / was** lots of fun.

☐ Total: 15

## Vocabulary builder

**6** (Circle) the correct options.

1 When they heard the scream, they were all ___ .

   **a** exciting  **b** terrified  **c** worrying

2 It's really important to take a ___ on a walk just in case of accidents.

   **a** first aid kit  **b** pen-knife  **c** sun cream

3 We decided to ___ really early in the morning because it was a long journey.

   **a** look round  **b** chill out  **c** set off

4 I would never go ___ because I'm afraid of heights.

   **a** sailing  **b** climbing  **c** theme park

5 Don't forget to ___ the lights. We're trying to save electricity.

   **a** turn down  **b** reduce  **c** switch off

6 I really like the new ___ in the middle of the square outside the art gallery.

   **a** sculpture  **b** portrait  **c** mural

7 It wasn't difficult to ___ new friends when I moved to my new school.

   **a** make  **b** know  **c** do

8 That's a really pretty ___ . Are you wearing it to the wedding?

   **a** flat shoes  **b** tight jeans  **c** flowery dress

9 That walk yesterday was great but really ___ . I went to bed early.

   **a** interested  **b** tiring  **c** boring

10 How can you ___ so much electricity? Be more careful!

   **a** save  **b** waste  **c** leave on

11 Are you interested ___ joining the gym?

   **a** on  **b** about  **c** in

☐ Total: 10

## Speaking

**7** **Complete the conversation with the phrases in the box.**

> don't fit   look great   ~~my size~~
> suits you   the changing rooms
> these shoes

**Nik:** I need a dress and some shoes for the party. Let's have a look.

**Amy:** Do you like this dress?

**Nik:** Oh, yes, it's really pretty, and it's ¹_____ *my size* _____ , too.

**Amy:** How about ²_____ ? They're perfect for a party.

**Nik:** Wow, yes. OK, I need to try everything on. Where are ³_____ ?

**Amy:** I think they're on the left at the back. Come on.
…

**Nik:** So, what do you think?

**Amy:** Oh the dress really ⁴_____ . And the shoes ⁵_____ , too!

**Nik:** Yes, but they ⁶_____ very well! They're a bit tight.

**Amy:** That's a pity. Well, just buy the dress then. There's a fantastic shoe shop near here. We can go there next.

☐ Total: 5

☐ Total: 56

## *used to* or *use to*?

Remember that:
- we use *used to* + infinitive to talk about past habits and states in affirmative sentences.
  - ✓ Punks **used to wear** dog collars as necklaces.
  - ✗ Punks *use to* wear dog collars as necklaces.
- we use *did(n't)* + subject + *use to* without the 'd' in questions.
  - ✓ **Did you use to** walk to school on your own?
  - ✗ *Did you used to* walk to school on your own?
- we use *did(n't)* + *use to* without the 'd' in negative sentences.
  - ✓ They **didn't use to** spend a lot of money on clothes.
  - ✗ They *didn't used to* spend a lot of money on clothes.

**1 Complete the sentences with *used to* or *use to*.**

1 My mum ___used to___ wear flowery dresses.
2 They didn't _____ wear a uniform.
3 Did you _____ be friends with Marco?
4 We _____ go to the same school.
5 She _____ come to my house on Saturdays.
6 How often did you _____ read fashion magazines?
7 I didn't _____ like him, but now we're good friends.
8 My brother _____ have long hair and wear make-up.

## Past perfect

Remember that:
- we use *had* + past participle to form the past perfect. Don't forget to use *had*!
  - ✓ I **had** never **been** to a live concert before the concert last week.
  - ✗ I *never been* to a live concert before the concert last week.
- we use the **past perfect** to talk about an action that happened **before** another action. We use the **past simple** to talk about the **most recent** of two actions.
  - ✓ When I **arrived**, Joe **had already gone** home.
  - ✗ When I arrived, *Joe already went* home.
  - ✗ When I *had* arrived, Joe had already gone home.

**2 Are the sentences correct? Correct the incorrect sentences.**

1 Rory never been camping before. He loved it!
   *Rory had never been camping before. He loved it!*
2 She had just started to do her homework when the phone rang.
   _____
3 Sarah saw that Julian forgot his keys.
   _____
4 We had to walk to school because our dad was sold the car.
   _____
5 She was happy because she always wanted to meet him.
   _____
6 They arrived at the concert late because they had got lost.
   _____
7 They ate all the pizza before we had arrived.
   _____
8 The dog was afraid because it was heard fireworks.
   _____

## Clothes

Remember that:
- *clothes* are things like dresses and trousers that cover our body. A *cloth* is a piece of material we use for cleaning things. Don't confuse *clothes* and *cloth*.
  - ✓ I've just bought some new **clothes**.
  - ✗ I've just bought some new *cloths*.
  - ✓ Clean the glasses with a soft **cloth**.
- *clothes* is always plural. It does not have a singular form without *-s* and we do not say 'a clothe' or 'a clothes'.
  - ✓ I like having new **clothes** to wear.
  - ✗ I like having *a new clothe* to wear.
- we use the verb *wear* to talk about having some clothes on our body. Don't say *use*.
  - ✓ I like **wearing** shorts in the summer.
  - ✗ I like *using* shorts in the summer.

**3 Find and correct five more mistakes in these sentences.**

1 I love ~~using~~ ‸ jeans! They're so comfortable. *(wearing)*
2 I bought a dress from the new cloth shop in my town.
3 I'm not interested in clothe and I don't like shopping.
4 I don't spend a lot of money on clothes.
5 You should use old clothes because we're going to paint my bedroom.
6 What kind of clothes do you like wearing?
7 My sister always wears a fashionable clothes.
8 People usually wear traditional cloths for weddings.

# 2 A helping hand

## Vocabulary
### Personal qualities

**1** ★ **Find nine more personal qualities in the wordsquare.**

| i | e | a | s | y | g | o | i | n | g | h | t |
|---|---|---|---|---|---|---|---|---|---|---|---|
| m | p | r | e | d | s | u | b | a | n | a | a |
| p | a | l | s | e | t | y | p | e | i | r | l |
| a | s | m | o | t | i | v | a | t | e | d | s |
| t | s | r | w | e | a | s | h | c | i | w | o |
| i | i | o | n | r | s | h | y | s | t | o | c |
| e | o | p | v | m | s | e | n | t | e | r | i |
| n | n | s | a | i | i | v | a | r | m | k | a |
| t | a | l | e | n | t | e | d | i | r | i | b |
| n | t | u | s | e | a | w | o | c | i | n | l |
| d | e | d | y | d | r | i | c | t | y | g | e |

**2** ★ **Complete the definitions with the words in Exercise 1.**

1 When you really want to do something, you're
  _motivated_ .
2 When you want everything to happen quickly,
  you're _____ .
3 When you have a special ability for something,
  you're _____ .
4 When you're relaxed about everything, you're
  _____ .
5 When you make sure that rules are never broken,
  you're _____ .
6 When you like meeting people, you're
  _____ .
7 When you work a lot, you're _____ .
8 When you're not confident around people, you're
  _____ .
9 When you have strong feelings about something,
  you're _____ about it.
10 When you never give up, you're _____ .

**3** ★★ **Complete the sentences with words from Exercise 1.**

1 Our History teacher is great. She's really
  _passionate_ about history and she makes it real.
2 I think you're really _____ . Why don't you
  enter the competition? I'm sure you can win!
3 His parents are quite _____ and are never
  angry when he gets home late.
4 He's so _____ . He studies for hours every
  day, doing the homework and then extra!
5 Athletes need to be very _____ to go out
  training when it's cold and wet.
6 I don't mind waiting five minutes in a shop, but I
  get _____ if I have to wait for a long time.

**4** ★★ **Complete the text with personal qualities.**

Laura, one of the girls in my class, is very ¹___shy___ .
She doesn't usually say much and, because she isn't
very ²_____ , she hasn't got a lot of friends.
So everyone was surprised when she got a big
part in the school play. We soon discovered why
though, she's really ³_____ about acting, and
a different person on stage. The drama teacher, Mrs
Martin, is quite ⁴_____ and most people are
scared of her. If you can't remember your words,
she can be quite ⁵_____ , and gets angry very
quickly! Laura, though, is very ⁶_____ . She
learned her part quickly and did extra practice, so Mrs
Martin was very pleased. Laura was amazing in the
play – she's so ⁷_____ , the best actress in the
school! Now she says she wants to be a professional
actress when she leaves school, and Mrs Martin is
helping her. She seems really ⁸_____ .

**5** ★★★ **Which of the adjectives describe you? Why? Write at least five sentences.**

*I'm very determined. Learning to skateboard was difficult but I did it!*

# Language focus 1

## Reflexive pronouns and *each other*

**1** ★ **Complete the tables with reflexive pronouns.**

Singular

| I | you | he | she | it |
|---|-----|----|----|----|
|   |     | *himself* |    |    |

Plural

| we | you | they |
|----|-----|------|
|    |     |      |

**2** ★ **Complete the sentences with the correct reflexive pronoun.**

1 I'm making ___myself___ a sandwich.
2 Karen cut _____ on some broken glass on the beach.
3 We really enjoyed _____ at the party. Thanks!
4 They bought _____ some new clothes in the sales.
5 My computer turns _____ off to save energy when I don't use it.
6 Here's the pizza, everyone! You can all help _____ .
7 He hurt _____ quite badly when he fell off his bike.
8 Wow! Did you do that all by _____ or did someone else help you?

**3** ★ **Complete the sentences in the table.**

| 1 | When John looks at John in the mirror, we say he looks at _____ . |
|---|---|
| 2 | When Annie texts Kate and Kate texts Annie, we say they text _____ . |

**4** ★★ (Circle) **the correct words.**

1 My friends and I always help **ourselves /** (**each other**) when we have a problem.
2 Did you enjoy **yourselves / each other** at the amusement park?
3 Harry taught **himself / each other** to play the guitar.
4 My best friend and I text **ourselves / each other** a lot when we go on holiday.
5 Luckily, Paula didn't hurt **herself / each other** when she fell off her bike.
6 They go to different schools but they see **themselves / each other** at the weekend.

**5** ★★ **Complete the postcard with reflexive pronouns and *each other*.**

Dear Mum and Dad,
Are you enjoying ¹ _yourselves_ without us?! It was a bit boring here with Granny and Granddad at first. There's no Internet, so we had to find ² _____ things to do. Joey has taught ³ _____ to skateboard, and I'm making ⁴ _____ a jumper for the winter – Granny's showing me how.
Nice surprise though – I saw Marie yesterday! We hadn't seen ⁵ _____ since we were little. We spent ages telling ⁶ _____ all our news – I was late for supper! Her parents have built ⁷ _____ a house here, so we can entertain ⁸ _____ all summer.
See you soon!
Love
Patri

**6** ★★★ **Write answers to the questions.**

1 How do you and your friends enjoy yourselves?
_____
2 Did you teach yourself to read?
_____
3 When do your family give each other presents?
_____
4 What do your friends do to stop themselves getting bored?
_____
5 What do you and your classmates help each other with?
_____

*We enjoy ourselves by playing video games.*

## Explore word building

**7** ★★ **Complete the second sentence with the related adjective or noun.**

1 She's very **determined**.
She's got a lot of ___determination___ .
2 He sings with so much **passion**!
He's really _____ about singing.
3 To be a gymnast, you need to be **flexible**.
You need a lot of _____ to be a gymnast.
4 Going on holiday makes me **happy**.
My idea of _____ is going on holiday.
5 Climbing that mountain is quite a **challenge**.
That mountain is quite _____ to climb.
6 His first album was an immediate **success**.
His first album was immediately _____ .

# Listening and vocabulary

## Listening

**1** ★ 🔊 **02** **Listen to an interview with a sprinter called Errol Dixon. Why is he unusual?**

a He is blind.

b He runs a lot of races.

c He races with another runner.

**2** ★★ 🔊 **02** **Listen again and choose the correct options.**

1 A guide runner …
   ⓐ helps a blind runner in races.
   b only runs with other sprinters.

2 Liz Stevens …
   a was born blind.
   b runs at more than one distance.

3 The most important thing for a guide runner is …
   a helping the other runner in training.
   b moving their arms and legs with the other runner.

4 Errol and Liz …
   a are joined together in a race.
   b don't need to think when they race.

5 Errol and Liz talk …
   a at the beginning of the race.
   b during every race.

6 Errol became a guide runner …
   a through a family member.
   b after he was in the Olympics in Beijing.

7 Errol and Liz …
   a have been together since they met in Beijing.
   b want to compete in the Paralympics.

8 Errol explains that he and Liz …
   a won a gold medal at London 2012.
   b both get a gold medal if they win.

## Phrasal verbs (learning and socialising)

**3** ★ **Complete the phrasal verbs with the prepositions in the box.**

| up up up up with together |
| on on on to |

1 create something new — set __up__

2 join a class or other organised activity — sign _____

3 respect someone — look _____ _____

4 teach or give new information — pass _____

5 depend on someone — count _____

6 have a good relationship with someone — get _____ _____

7 stop doing something — give _____

8 help people be friendly to each other — bring _____

**4** ★★ **Complete the sentences with the phrasal verbs from Exercise 3.**

1 If you need any help, just ask. You can always __count on__ me.

2 My granny's teaching me to cook. She says it's important to _____ her skills.

3 I really _____ my next-door neighbour. She's 72, but she's a good friend.

4 They are planning to _____ a chess club at school this term. I wanted all my friends to _____ , but most of them weren't interested!

5 Joey decided to _____ football, because all the training sessions were too much with schoolwork.

6 We hope to _____ old and young people to help each other with this new project.

7 Young people often _____ sports people or musicians.

# Language focus 2

## Present perfect simple

**1** ★ (Circle) the correct words in the table.

| | |
|---|---|
| 1 | We can use the present perfect simple to talk about a series of actions in the **past / present**. |
| 2 | We often use the present perfect simple to ask about **how many / how long**. |

**2** ★★ Write present perfect simple sentences with the prompts.

1 pieces of pizza / you / eat?
_How many pieces of pizza have you eaten?_

2 She / win / a lot of competitions
_____

3 We / make / three cakes for the party
_____

4 times / they / go / there?
_____

5 I / send / 100 texts / this week
_____

6 people / he / invite / to the birthday party?
_____

## Present perfect continuous

**3** ★ Complete the rules in the table.

| | |
|---|---|
| 1 | We use the present perfect continuous to refer to a time period that _____ finished. |
| 2 | We often use the present perfect continuous to ask about how _____ . |
| 3 | We can use the present perfect continuous to refer to actions we expect to _____ in the future. |

**4** ★★ Complete the sentences with the present perfect continuous form of the verbs in the box.

| look   run   practise   ~~come~~   go   work |
|---|

1 My family _____ *has been coming* _____ to this campsite for ten years.

2 She _____ the piano every night for the concert.

3 We _____ on our project every weekend for weeks.

4 My parents _____ for a new car for weeks.

5 I _____ to the youth club for two months. It's great!

6 David _____ in races since he was 10.

## Present perfect simple vs. present perfect continuous

**5** ★★★ Your friend Callum does a lot of work with a charity. Answer the questions with full sentences using the words in brackets.

1 How many people have visited your charity's website this year, Callum? (about 100,000)
_About 100,000 people have visited our website._

2 How long have you been doing charity work? (every Saturday for two years)
_____

3 What activities have you been doing this year to make money? (parachute jumps and quizzes)
_____

4 How many parachute jumps have you organised? (four so far)
_____

5 Who has the charity been helping this year? (groups of children all over the country)
_____

6 How many children has the charity helped? (thousands)
_____

**6** ★★★ Write questions with the present perfect simple and continuous. Answer them for you.

1 How many / films / you / watch / this week?
_____
_____

2 How long / you / come / this school?
_____
_____

3 you / learn English / a long time?
_____
_____

4 How many times / you / look / your mobile phone / today?
_____
_____

_How many films have you watched this week?_
_I haven't watched any!_

# Reading

**1** ★ **Read the article about Lady Gaga's charity. What is the charity's message?**

a 'Different is best'

b 'Accept individual differences'

c 'Singing is good for you'

# BORN THIS WAY

Stefani Germanotta, better known as Lady Gaga, is famous for her extravagant style. She has always been different, and she says that's why she was bullied when she was at secondary school. Gaga has told the media that other pupils *made fun of* her for being ugly, being fat, having a big nose, being annoying, having a funny laugh and being *weird*. She was also constantly asked why she always sang, why she was so keen on theatre and why she did her make-up the way she did. Gaga has said that sometimes it got so bad she didn't even want to go to school.

Since then Lady Gaga has become rich, famous and successful for some of the things she was once bullied about, so she decided to try and help young people who found themselves in the situation she was in at school. In 2011, she and her mother Cynthia started a non-profit organisation called the Born This Way Foundation, (BTWF). Its aim is to build a society where people accept each other's differences and individuality. Gaga wants to bring young people together to create a new kind of community, based on three things: safety, and the skills and opportunities to make a kinder, braver world.

For many teenagers who are bullied, home is no escape because the *bullying* continues online. Lady Gaga has met Barack Obama to discuss action against cyber-bullying, and also demands more *moderators* on social media sites.

BTWF has been helping young people to set up 'Born Brave' school and community groups. The aim of these is to encourage young people to be more *tolerant*. The charity wants everyone to feel safe in their community, school, home, wherever they live, and to develop the skills they need to live in peace with other people.

**2** ★★ **Match the words in bold in the text with the definitions.**

1 accepting that people are different _____

2 say horrible things about _____

3 people who delete bad comments on social media sites _____

4 being cruel to or hurting someone weaker _____

5 strange or unusual _____

**3** ★★ **Read the first paragraph again. Complete the table with the reasons why Lady Gaga was bullied.**

| Appearance | Personality | Interests | Behaviour |
|---|---|---|---|
| ugly | | | |

**4** ★★★ **Now read the rest of the article again. Complete the notes about the charity.**

BT
WF

Name: ¹ _the Born This Way Foundation_

Started: in ² _____ by
³ _____

Aim: ⁴ _____

Idea is: to create a community with
⁵ _____ , ⁶ _____ and ⁷ _____
to make the world better

Charity also wants: to stop ⁸ _____ bullying
on ⁹ _____ sites

'Born Brave' groups: work with ¹⁰ _____
people in their ¹¹ _____ and ¹²  _____

**5** ★★★ **What do you think of Lady Gaga's charity? Is it necessary where you live? Why/Why not? Write at least five sentences.**

# Writing

## A personal email

**1** **Read Olivia's email. Why is she writing to Sophie?**

> ✉ *Your*MAIL ⊕ New Reply | ▼ Delete Junk | ▼
>
> Dear Sophie,
>
> I'm writing to say thank you for all the help you gave me when my family and I came to live in Dublin. Going to live in another city was very difficult and at the beginning I ¹ _found_ Dublin so strange compared to the neighbourhood where you and I lived in Liverpool. I also ² _____ really different from everyone here but your advice to sign up for lots of after-school activities really helped. I've been learning a bit of Irish, which I ³ _____ really confusing, and I'm learning to play the guitar. I'm determined to make more friends and to be more sociable.
>
> Speaking to each other on Skype™ is great and all those amazing messages you've been sending me are really motivating. It's been great to be able to count on you when I'm ⁴ _____ lonely. I've made a few friends and now I'm ⁵ _____ life here much easier. I've been telling them all about you. I hope you come and visit soon.
>
> Anyway, thanks again for everything. You're a great friend.
>
> Lots of love,
>
> Olivia

**2** **Read the email again. Answer the questions.**

1 Where does Olivia live now?
   *She lives in Dublin.*

2 How does she know Sophie?
   _____

3 What advice did Sophie give Olivia?
   _____

4 What after-school activities is Olivia doing?
   _____

5 How do Olivia and Sophie contact each other?
   _____

6 How has Olivia's life changed since she followed Sophie's advice?
   _____

**Useful language** Expressing how we feel ——————

**3** **Complete Olivia's email with the correct form of *feel* or *find*.**

**4** **Write sentences with *feel* or *find* and your own ideas.**

1 learning English / difficult
   *I find learning English very difficult.*

2 shy / I first came to this school
   _____

3 Maths / difficult at the beginning
   _____

4 determined / get on with my new friends
   _____

5 meeting new people / hard
   _____

6 motivated / try new things
   _____

**5** **Rewrite the sentences using an *-ing* form at the beginning.**

1 It wasn't as difficult to make new friends as I thought.
   *Making new friends wasn't as difficult as*
   *I thought.*

2 It is always easier for you to meet new people after school.
   _____

3 It was a wonderful experience to bring all my friends together.
   _____

4 It has been great fun to go to swimming classes with you.
   _____

5 I've been writing a diary and that's been very useful.
   _____

# Writing

**6** (Circle) **the correct words.**

1 At first, I felt really (bored)/ boring all the time.
2 At the beginning, I found your advice really motivated / motivating.
3 I wasn't very worried / worrying about missing so many swimming lessons.
4 I've always found History very confused / confusing – so many dates!
5 I felt a bit depressed / depressing about moving to another city.
6 It's been really amazed / amazing to make new friends.

> **WRITING TIP**
>
> Make it better! ✓ ✓ ✓
> In your email, put in some sentences which talk directly to the person you are writing to.
> *You have helped me so much, you're the best friend I could wish for.*

**7 Read the sentences. Which one does <u>not</u> talk directly to the reader?**

1 You know how impatient I can be.
2 You've been such a great help to me over the last few months.
3 Getting these messages has been very important to me.
4 I always felt really determined after talking to you.
5 You're such an easy-going person and a really good friend.

**8 Put the information in the order it appears in Olivia's email in Exercise 1.**

> how she felt about the changes in her life
> why she's writing
> how her friend helped her
> say thank you
> what she's doing to solve her problems
> how her life has changed

1 *why she's writing*
2 _____
3 _____
4 _____
5 _____
6 _____

## PLAN

**9 You are going to write a thank you email to a friend or family member who gave you advice in a difficult situation. Choose one of the situations below. Use the categories in Exercise 8 and make notes.**

- You were having a lot of trouble with a subject at school.
- You did an exchange with a student in another country.
- You were often bored after school.
- You were finding concentrating on your homework very difficult.

## WRITE

**10 Write your thank you email. Look at page 27 of the Student's Book to help you.**

_____
_____
_____
_____
_____
_____
_____
_____
_____
_____
_____
_____
_____
_____
_____
_____
_____
_____

## CHECK

**11 Check your writing. Can you say YES to these questions?**

- Have you used the ideas in Exercise 8?
- Have you used *feel* and *find* to express your feelings?
- Have you written a sentence with an *-ing* form at the beginning?
- Have you used *-ed* and *-ing* adjectives correctly?
- Have you used some sentences which talk directly to the reader?
- Are the spelling and punctuation correct?

**Do you need to write a second draft?**

# Vocabulary
## Personal qualities

**1 Match the sentences (1–6) with the sentences (a–f) that follow them.**

1 My sister's so **impatient**. _b_
2 Janie's parents are quite **strict**. ___
3 I'm not feeling very **sociable** today. ___
4 She's really **motivated**. ___
5 She's too **easy-going**. ___
6 Your parents are very **hard-working**. ___

a I don't want to go to the party.
b She hates waiting, everything has to happen now!
c They both work long hours in the restaurant.
d She always does what other people want to do.
e They don't let her come out with us very often.
f She practises a lot more than the rest of us.

Total: 5

## Phrasal verbs (learning and socialising)

**2 Circle the correct phrasal verbs.**

Many young people, especially boys, ¹**look up to** / **get on with** professional footballers. Some players use the relationship they have with their fans to help them ²**pass on** / **give up** anti-social behaviour, and find a job. They try to ³**pass on** / **bring together** their own life experiences and sometimes ⁴**give up** / **set up** their own charities to ⁵**bring together** / **look up to** boys and girls from different neighbourhoods. These young people can ⁶**count on** / **sign up** for sports activities, educational courses or job training.

Total: 5

# Language focus
## Reflexive pronouns and *each other*

**3 Complete the conversations with reflexive pronouns or *each other*.**

**Nina:** Great party, Sue. Everyone's enjoying ¹ _themselves_ !
**Sue:** Thanks! Hey guys! There's lots of food in the kitchen. Just help ²_____ !

**Jake:** Did you teach ³_____ to play the guitar? I tried to teach ⁴_____ once, but I couldn't do it!
**Kim:** Well, Gary was teaching ⁵_____ at the same time, so we helped ⁶_____ .

Total: 5

# Present perfect simple

**4 Write present perfect simple sentences.**

1 We / learn / a lot of things / in Biology / this term
_We've learned a lot of things in Biology this term._
2 How many / text messages / you / send / today?
_____
3 They / win / several awards / for their charity work
_____
4 I / not have / any exams / this month
_____
5 How many / times / she / go / to the youth club?
_____
6 He / help / a lot of people / with problems
_____

Total: 5

# Present perfect continuous

**5 Complete the sentences with the present perfect continuous form of the verbs in the box.**

give   not go   come   help   ~~visit~~   make

1 You _'ve been visiting_ _____ him a lot recently.
2 How long _____ you _____ to class?
3 She _____ to the extra Maths classes but she should.
4 They _____ cakes all day.
5 He _____ his elderly neighbours to do their shopping.
6 _____ you _____ money to the Animal Rescue Centre?

Total: 5

# Present perfect simple vs. present perfect continuous

**6 Complete the sentences with the correct form of the verbs in brackets.**

1 We ___ _have raised_ ___ (raise) £500 for charity.
2 He _____ (go) to the football club for nearly a year now.
3 You look really tired! How many exams _____ (have) this week?
4 I _____ (not sell) any tickets for the charity concert. Nobody's interested!
5 We _____ (pick) up rubbish from the beach every weekend since May.
6 How long _____ (they/help) at the youth club on Friday evenings?

Total: 5

## Language builder

**7** (Circle) the correct options.

**Cath:** ¹___ did you live before, Ned?

**Ned:** We ²___ live in the city centre. I loved it!

**Cath:** Why ³___ here, then?

**Ned:** Well, my granny ⁴___ ill in hospital, and after she got better she found it difficult to look after ⁵___ . We ⁶___ her in the summer holidays each year, but of course, that wasn't enough, so my parents decided to move near her.

**Cath:** ⁷___ this cottage? It's beautiful.

**Ned:** My parents ⁸___ home from my granny's house one weekend when they ⁹___ it. We only moved in a few days ago, that's why all our things are still in boxes! Those boxes are all my parents' books.

**Cath:** Wow, what a lot! How many books ¹⁰___ with them?

**Ned:** I've got no idea, hundreds, I suppose, but we ¹¹___ boxes ever since we arrived. We've got so much stuff that I ¹²___ found all my things!

| | **a** | **b** | **c** |
|---|---|---|---|
| **1** | ⓐ Where | **b** When | **c** What |
| **2** | **a** would | **b** had | **c** used to |
| **3** | **a** you came | **b** did you come | **c** had you come |
| **4** | **a** had been | **b** has been | **c** had |
| **5** | **a** himself | **b** each other | **c** herself |
| **6** | **a** didn't use to visit | **b** have visited | **c** would visit |
| **7** | **a** Who did you find | **b** Who found | **c** Who did find |
| **8** | **a** drove | **b** were driving | **c** had driven |
| **9** | **a** had seen | **b** were seeing | **c** saw |
| **10** | **a** had they brought | **b** have they brought | **c** have they been bringing |
| **11** | **a** 've unpacked | **b** 've been unpacking | **c** were unpacking |
| **12** | **a** yet haven't | **b** haven't already | **c** still haven't |

Total: 11

## Vocabulary builder

**8** (Circle) the correct options.

**1** We were ___ by the small amount of money we raised. We'd expected more.

　ⓐ disappointed　**b** proud　**c** fascinated

**2** I can't go camping. I haven't got a ___ .

　**a** sleeping bag　**b** water bottle　**c** pen-knife

**3** She loves running. I've never known anyone so ___ about their sport.

　**a** shy　**b** passionate　**c** easy-going

**4** The karaoke was fun, but using a ___ isn't as easy as it looks.

　**a** gallery　**b** microphone　**c** juggler

**5** I need to quickly make ___ . Is that OK?

　**a** a mess　**b** my homework　**c** a phone call

**6** I went on the Internet to ___ when the concert was.

　**a** pick up　**b** find out　**c** look up to

**7** More people are ___ of the dark than you think.

　**a** keen　**b** afraid　**c** happy

**8** I'd like to go ___ next weekend but there isn't any snow at the moment.

　**a** sailing　**b** trekking　**c** skiing

**9** He was a ___ footballer but too lazy to do much training.

　**a** motivated　**b** strict　**c** talented

**10** Those are nice boots. Are they made of ___ ?

　**a** leather　**b** silk　**c** flat

Total: 9

## Speaking

**9** **Put the sentences in the correct order to make a conversation.**

_1_ **A:** What's up Pam? You don't look very happy.

___ **A:** I know what you mean. Look, you don't need to worry. Just don't use your phone much if she's there. She'll soon forget.

___ **A:** Oh, you poor thing! What was it about?

___ **A:** Look, I'm sure she'll calm down soon. She always does.

___ **A:** Right! I'm sure it will be fine. Now, how can I make you feel better? Shall we go to the sports centre?

___ **B:** Yes, I suppose you're right. That's what happened last time!

___ **B:** Well, she doesn't realise how important my phone is. I'd be lost without it!

___ **B:** She says I use my phone too much, and she doesn't want to pay for it.

___ **B:** I've had another argument with my mum.

Total: 8

Total: 58

# ⊙ Get it right! Unit 2

## Reflexive pronouns

Remember that:
- we use reflexive pronouns when the object of the verb is the same as the subject. We do not use object pronouns.
  - ✓ I enjoyed the concert.
  - ✓ I enjoyed **myself** (at the concert).
  - ✗ I enjoyed ~~me~~ (at the concert).
- when a reflexive pronoun refers to more than one person, we use -**selves**, not -**selfs**.
  - ✓ Did the boys enjoy **themselves** at the concert?
  - ✗ Did the boys enjoy ~~themselfs~~ at the concert?

**1 Complete the conversation with the correct pronouns. Check your spelling!**

**Rob:** Hi Mary, did you enjoy ¹ ___yourself___ last weekend?

**Mary:** Well, it was OK. I went for a picnic with my friends on Saturday.

**Rob:** That sounds good!

**Mary:** Yes, but my friend Helen just talked about ² _____ all the time. I was bored.

**Rob:** What did you do on Sunday?

**Mary:** We went to play tennis, one of my brothers hurt ³ _____ and we had to go home. My parents were out, so we had to look after ⁴ _____ . I cooked dinner, and my brothers taught ⁵ _____ to play a new video game.

**Rob:** Do you want to go to the cinema next weekend? That would be fun!

**Mary:** OK. Thanks! I'll see you next weekend. Bye!

**Rob:** Take care of ⁶ _____ . Bye!

## advice

Remember that:
- *advice* is an uncountable noun. It does not have a plural form with -*s* and we do not use *a/an* before it.
  - ✓ I'm writing to thank you for your **advice** about my new school.
  - ✗ I'm writing to thank you for your ~~advices~~ about my new school.
  - ✓ My mum always gives me good **advice**.
  - ✗ My mum always gives me ~~a~~ good advice.
- *advice* is the noun, but the verb is **advise**.
  - ✓ He **advised** me to take the train to London.
  - ✗ He ~~adviced~~ me to take the train to London.
  - ✓ Thank you for your **advice**.
  - ✗ Thank you for your ~~advise~~.

**2 Find and correct five more mistakes with *advice* in the email.**

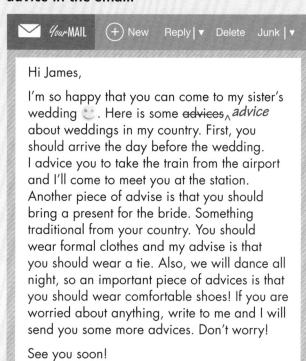

Hi James,

I'm so happy that you can come to my sister's wedding 😊. Here is some ~~advices~~∧ *advice* about weddings in my country. First, you should arrive the day before the wedding. I advice you to take the train from the airport and I'll come to meet you at the station. Another piece of advise is that you should bring a present for the bride. Something traditional from your country. You should wear formal clothes and my advise is that you should wear a tie. Also, we will dance all night, so an important piece of advices is that you should wear comfortable shoes! If you are worried about anything, write to me and I will send you some more advices. Don't worry!

See you soon!

Maria

**Spell it right!** Personal qualities

B1 and B2 students often make spelling mistakes when writing these adjectives for personal qualities from Unit 2. Remember to write them correctly.

hard-working    easy-going    sociable

strict    talented    (im)patient

**3 Correct the spelling mistake in each sentence.**

1 She's a very ~~hard worker~~∧ *hard-working* person and she practises every day.

2 They're a very tallented family – they all play a musical instrument.

3 Jane's a successful businesswoman and very hard working.

4 Her parents are very social. They've been out every night this week!

5 My teacher is sometimes impacient with us when we don't know the answers.

6 He's a very easy going person and always great fun.

7 My parents are quite strickt about what time I go to bed.

# ③ Young achievers

## Vocabulary

### Training and qualifications

**1** ⭐ **Put the sections in the correct order to make a text.**

a Most young people don't know what they want to do in life. Often finding a **career**

b **fees**, but they didn't have much money, so I decided to try and look for a **part-time**

c **exam**, but I passed and I've been a museum curator ever since!

d **path** is more luck than anything, I think. When I left school, I started a **university**

e **form**. The course only had twenty places, and to be accepted I had to take an **entrance**

f **experience** for a historian and I loved it. Then the director suggested doing a **training**

g **degree** in History, my favourite subject at school. My parents agreed to pay the **course**

h **course** to be a museum curator. It sounded interesting, so I filled in the **application**

i **job**. I was lucky. I got a job at the local museum giving guided tours. It was great **work**

1 _a_   2 ___   3 ___   4 ___   5 ___
6 ___   7 ___   8 ___   9 ___

**2** ⭐⭐ **Complete the sentences. Use one or two words from Exercise 1 for each space.**

1 I can't decide if I want to go to __university__ and study for a degree, or try and find a job.

2 When do I have to pay the _____ for next year?

3 It says on your _____ that you have always been interested in computers.

4 That university has a(n) _____ exam and it's really difficult to get a place there.

5 I see you've done language _____ in French, Dutch and Spanish. How fluent are you?

6 She's had so many different jobs it's difficult to see a clear career _____ .

**3** ⭐⭐ **Complete the job advert.**

---

### Secondary school teachers needed

HIGHLANDS · HIGHLANDS

We need both ¹ __full-time__ (40 hours a week) and ² _____ teachers (15 or 21 hours a week) for the next academic year. The ³ _____ is challenging and interesting, and every day is different. Teaching is a(n) ⁴ _____ where you can really make a difference!

**Qualifications:**
You need a teacher ⁵ _____ certificate in the subject you want to teach. Some ⁶ _____ working with children in a school environment is also an advantage, as is a university ⁷ _____ .

**Applications:**
Please download and complete the ⁸ _____ by visiting our webpage.

---

**4** ⭐⭐⭐ **Look at the jobs in the box. What do people need to do them in your country? How many words from Exercise 1 can you use?**

> car mechanic   dentist   secondary school teacher
> radio presenter   hotel receptionist   pilot

*To be a dentist, you need a university degree and a year of practical experience.*

# Language focus 1

## *be going to* and present tenses for the future

**1** ⭐ Circle the correct options.

1 What time **are you meeting** / do you meet your friends at the library?

2 The exam tomorrow **is going to start / starts** at 8.30 am.

3 My sister **is going to do / is doing** work experience before her degree if she can.

4 The Young People of the Year Awards **take / are going to take** place this Friday.

5 Nathan **is going / is going to go** for a job interview this afternoon. He's very nervous!

6 No, we **aren't going / don't go** to see each other until Sunday.

7 I've decided **I'm studying / I'm going to study** computer science at university.

8 What day **does school finish / is school going to finish** this term?

**2** ⭐⭐ Complete the text with the correct future form of the verbs in brackets.

### LUCA, BASKETBALL PLAYER, ARGENTINA, 14

Q: **What are you doing at the weekend?**

A: I [1] *'m playing*_____ (play) a league match on Saturday morning, and I [2]_____ (go) to a party with some friends in the evening. On Sunday, I [3]_____ (not do) a lot. I [4]_____ (relax).

Q: **And what are your plans for the summer?**

A: In July, my team [5]_____ (take) part in an international tournament in Spain. It [6]_____ (start) at the end of June and [7]_____ (end) in early August.

Q: **So, what about your future, Luca?**

A: That's easy! I [8]_____ (work) hard and one day I [9]_____ (play) in the NBA.

**3** ⭐⭐⭐ Complete the text with the correct future form of the verbs in the box.

> study    practise    prepare    go    ~~compete~~
> not get    participate    take

Kaye Yao, 15, [1] __is competing__ in the South Korean Sudoku Super Challenge this year with thousands of other teenage competitors. The event [2]_____ place next December. Yao [3]_____ for the fourth time (last year she was third in her category). So, how [4]_____ she _____ for the championships? Well, she [5]_____ to a two-day training camp next November. Then she [6]_____ every day until the championships, but she [7]_____ nervous. 'I just do Sudoku for fun,' says Yao. 'I love logic and puzzles and I [8]_____ Maths at university.'

**4** ⭐⭐⭐ Write answers to the questions.

1 When is the next birthday in your family and whose is it?
_____

2 What are the dates of the next school holidays?
_____

3 What arrangements have you got in the next few weeks, and who with?
_____

4 What are your plans for the future?
_____

*My mum's birthday is on December 14th.*

## Explore expressions with *take*

**5** ⭐⭐ Complete the text with the words in the box.

> time    the exams    ~~place~~    advice    up

There's a big education fair in my city which takes [1] __place__ in May each year. I'm going to go because I don't know what to do when I leave school. It's difficult to know who to take [2]_____ from, because everyone tells me different things! Dad says I should take [3]_____ a job in the family business, like he did. My teachers think I should go to university, and Mum wants me to take [4]_____ to go to Oxford or Cambridge. I suppose I can take [5]_____ to decide what I want to do as I'm only 14, but I like to plan ahead!

# Listening and vocabulary

## Listening

**1** ★ 🔊 **03** **Listen to a journalist interviewing a child actress. Tick (✓) the plans Sarah has for the future.**

film acting ☐          stage acting ☐
writing ☐          a university course ☐

**2** ★★ 🔊 **03** **Listen again. Are these sentences true (*T*) or false (*F*)?**

1   Sarah made her first film when she was five.   _F_
2   She didn't enjoy being in films when she started.   ___
3   She wanted to go to high school and make friends.   ___
4   When she was in films, she had tutors and no friends her own age.   ___
5   She continued to have acting offers after she gave it up.   ___
6   After she stopped acting, she still wanted to be rich and famous.   ___
7   Her novel is about her problems with growing up.   ___
8   She often can't decide what she wants to do.   ___
9   She plans to write another novel.   ___
10  She acted in lots of student productions at school.   ___

## Achievements

**3** ★ **Match the verbs (1–8) with the words and phrases in the box.**

> records   project   fortune   voluntary work
> ~~business~~   community   millionaire   awards

1   start a _business_
2   break _____
3   win _____
4   support the _____
5   become a _____
6   develop a _____
7   do _____
8   make a _____

**4** ★★ **Complete the texts with the correct form of the expressions in Exercise 3.**

Usain Bolt worked hard to be a sprinter (his coach said he was too tall!), and won his first gold medal at 15. Since then he has ¹ ___*broken*___ the world ___*record*___ several times, and in the process he has ² _____ a multi-_____ . He now earns a salary of $20m a year, and though he doesn't have time to ³_____ any _____ himself, he has given millions of dollars to charity.

Nowadays, many young people are trying to ⁴_____ an online _____ , like Mark Zuckerberg did with Facebook. He ⁵_____ the _____ for a social-networking site with some friends at university, and it was so successful that by the age of 23 he had ⁶_____ . He's now a billionaire and Facebook has over a billion users.

Shakira, who had her first big hit in South America when she was only 19, has set up her own charity, Pies Descalzos, in Colombia. The charity ⁷_____ poor children in _____ , and helps them to get an education. In 2014, she ⁸_____ a Hero _____ at the Radio Disney Music Awards for her charity work.

# Language focus 2

## Predictions with *be going to, will* and *may/might*

**1** ★★ **Complete the predictions with the correct form of the verbs in brackets.**

1  You've done a fantastic project! You *'ll win* (win) an award, I'm sure.
2  Next year, we _____ (have) enough money to open another shop. I hope so!
3  Now she's in the last 100 metres – she _____ (break) the world record by several seconds! Amazing!
4  They are so creative. I'm sure they _____ (be) a success.
5  She's on the last chapter of her novel now. I think she _____ (finish) it this week.
6  They _____ (win) the league, but they're not the only good team. It _____ (not be) easy.
7  The way things are going with the business, we _____ (not make) a fortune.
8  He's a great actor. He _____ (get) an Oscar one day, I know.

## Future continuous

**2** ★ **Complete the rules in the table.**

| 1 | To form the future continuous, use *will* + _____ + _____ . |
|---|---|
| 2 | We use the future continuous to make _____ about the future. |
| 3 | We only use the future continuous with actions, not with _____ verbs. |

**3** ★★ **Complete the sentences with the future continuous form of the verbs in the box.**

| make   stay   do   not live   ~~study~~   work |
|---|

1  Next year, I *'ll be studying* at university in Paris, I hope.
2  My brother thinks he _____ a fortune soon. He's very ambitious.
3  In the future, more people _____ from home and sending emails to their bosses.
4  In a few years time, we _____ at home anymore.
5  _____ you _____ at school until you're 18?
6  If my application is successful, I _____ voluntary work in Africa next summer.

**4** ★★ **Join the parts of the sentences for each person.**

Adrian:
1  We don't think he's going                    *b*
2  He has lots of great ideas. He may         ___
3  Soon he'll be                                      ___

a  making a fortune, I'm sure.
b  to go to university. He wants to earn money.
c  try to develop one into an online business.

Gemma:
4  I think she's                                       ___
5  As a female student, she'll                    ___
6  She's not sure, but that                        ___

d  enter a world of male students, I suppose.
e  might feel strange after an all-girl's school.
f  going to study engineering at university.

**5** ★★ (Circle) **the correct options in the text.**

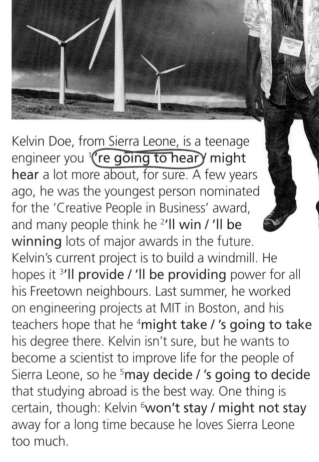

Kelvin Doe, from Sierra Leone, is a teenage engineer you [1]('re going to hear) / might hear a lot more about, for sure. A few years ago, he was the youngest person nominated for the 'Creative People in Business' award, and many people think he [2]'ll win / 'll be winning lots of major awards in the future. Kelvin's current project is to build a windmill. He hopes it [3]'ll provide / 'll be providing power for all his Freetown neighbours. Last summer, he worked on engineering projects at MIT in Boston, and his teachers hope that he [4]might take / 's going to take his degree there. Kelvin isn't sure, but he wants to become a scientist to improve life for the people of Sierra Leone, so he [5]may decide / 's going to decide that studying abroad is the best way. One thing is certain, though: Kelvin [6]won't stay / might not stay away for a long time because he loves Sierra Leone too much.

**6** ★★★ **Choose three of your friends. Make two predictions about each of them using the forms on this page.**

*Chloe might go and live abroad one day.*

# Reading

**1** ★ **Read the profiles of three teenagers and match them to their achievements.**

Angela ___    Santiago ___    Charley ___

a  sport
b  physics
c  computer coding
d  medical research
e  gaming
f  teaching

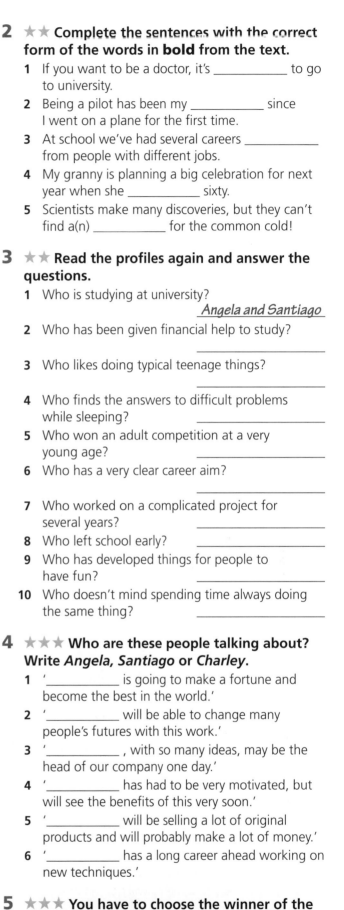

# TEENAGE
# ACHIEVERS

**Angela Zhang** recently finished high school in California, but she has already won a $100,000 award to study at university for her research on a nanoparticle system for treating cancer. Angela said she started developing the project in her first year at high school, reading bio-engineering articles and attending scientific *talks*. Later on, she did research in a laboratory at Stanford, where she successfully tested the system on mice. It might be years before we know if the system will work on humans, but she may be on the way to finding a *cure* for cancer. When she's not doing that, Angela is like any typical teenager. She loves buying shoes, and in her free time goes canoeing and walking.

**Santiago Gonzalez** is a 14-year-old computer scientist from Colorado, USA. He already attends university, and will graduate at 16, and complete his master's degree at 17. He's fluent in a dozen programming languages, and says that when he has a difficult programming problem, he will often dream the solution. Santiago happily calls himself a geek, and says that for him learning is as *essential* as eating. When he's not studying, he writes mobile apps. He's already developed about 15, including puzzles and games. His *ambition* is to work at Apple.

**Charley Hull** started playing golf when she was only 2, and was soon beating golfers much older than her. She had her first big success aged 9, when she won the English Amateur Ladies Championship. She started home schooling at 13 so she could travel to tournaments. In 2013, aged 17, Charley *turned* professional, and was voted the best new player, or 'rookie', of the European Tour. On the golf course, she's incredibly determined. Friends say, 'She's going to be world number 1!', and experts agree it may not take her very long. Off the golf course, she loves music, parties and being with her friends.

**2** ★★ **Complete the sentences with the correct form of the words in bold from the text.**

1  If you want to be a doctor, it's _____ to go to university.
2  Being a pilot has been my _____ since I went on a plane for the first time.
3  At school we've had several careers _____ from people with different jobs.
4  My granny is planning a big celebration for next year when she _____ sixty.
5  Scientists make many discoveries, but they can't find a(n) _____ for the common cold!

**3** ★★ **Read the profiles again and answer the questions.**

1  Who is studying at university?
    *Angela and Santiago*
2  Who has been given financial help to study?
    _____
3  Who likes doing typical teenage things?
    _____
4  Who finds the answers to difficult problems while sleeping?    _____
5  Who won an adult competition at a very young age?    _____
6  Who has a very clear career aim?
    _____
7  Who worked on a complicated project for several years?    _____
8  Who left school early?    _____
9  Who has developed things for people to have fun?    _____
10  Who doesn't mind spending time always doing the same thing?    _____

**4** ★★★ **Who are these people talking about? Write Angela, Santiago or Charley.**

1  '_____ is going to make a fortune and become the best in the world.'
2  '_____ will be able to change many people's futures with this work.'
3  '_____ , with so many ideas, may be the head of our company one day.'
4  '_____ has had to be very motivated, but will see the benefits of this very soon.'
5  '_____ will be selling a lot of original products and will probably make a lot of money.'
6  '_____ has a long career ahead working on new techniques.'

**5** ★★★ **You have to choose the winner of the 'Young Person of the Year Award'. Who do you think should win – Angela, Santiago or Charley – and why? Write at least five sentences.**

# Writing

## An opinion essay

**1** Read the essay. Does the author agree or disagree with the opinion in the essay title?

### School leavers should attend university before they start working. Do you agree?

The best students go to university. That's what everyone has always told us. [1]**Firstly, / However,** I don't think all school leavers should go to university before they start working.

[2]**In conclusion, / Firstly,** we have to ask ourselves why we would want to send all school leavers to do a university course. [3]**Although / However,** these courses can be very useful and students can learn a lot, not all students are capable of studying at the level required by universities to become scientists, teachers or lawyers. [4]**In addition, / Whereas** we also need people who are going to work in factories, repair machines or grow things for us to eat – important technical skills that don't require a degree.

Finally, [5]**in addition, / whereas** there are a lot of school leavers who want to continue studying at a higher level, there are many who would rather start working immediately or do training for a practical skill. Not everyone wants to go to university.

[6]**In conclusion, / In addition,** I don't agree that all school leavers should go to university. A degree is the logical path for many students, but it's definitely not the *only* path.

**2** Read the essay again. Tick (✓) the points the author makes.

1 Students can get a lot of knowledge from university courses. ✓
2 Not every school leaver wants to continue studying. ☐
3 Many school leavers don't have the correct academic level for university. ☐
4 Universities are often very expensive and not everyone can afford them. ☐
5 As well as professional people with university degrees, we also need people with other skills. ☐
6 Only university students will get the best jobs. ☐

**Useful language** Linking phrases

**3** Read the essay again. Circle the correct options.

**4** Complete this short essay with the linking phrases in the box.

> although   in conclusion   ~~firstly~~   in addition
> whereas   however

**Students should learn financial skills at school**

There are several points to consider. [1]___*Firstly*___ , it is an important life skill to learn how to make financial decisions. [2]_____ , we need to know what consequences our decisions about money will have. [3]_____ we handle money every day, many of us don't understand the value of money. Some people would argue we don't need to understand, [4]_____ others would say it's important to learn this early in life. [5]_____ , we cannot deny that basic financial skills can be important.

[6]_____ , I believe that financial skills should be learned from a young age.

# Writing

**5** Circle the correct options.

1 No / **Not** everyone wants to learn skills like these.
2 **Many** / Much students want to continue learning.
3 Lot / **Lots** of people want to find a job quickly.
4 Only few / **a few** school leavers will end up in top jobs.
5 All / **Every** schools want the best for their students.
6 **Some** / Any people believe that students should stay in school longer.

**6** Complete the sentences with the correct form of the verbs in the box.

> leave   think   ~~learn~~   study   do

1 Many students would rather do a training course or _____**learn**_____ a new skill.
2 Students have to make important decisions and _____ carefully.
3 Many people are going back to school or _____ courses.
4 Nowadays, most people study, whereas in the past many people got a job or _____ the country.
5 He didn't enjoy going to school or _____ .

> **WRITING TIP**
>
> Make it better! ✓ ✓ ✓
> Use different expressions to give your opinion.
> **I feel that** *work experience can often be more useful than formal training.*

**7** Circle the correct words.

1 To / **In** my opinion, children leave school too early.
2 I **believe** / opinion it's important to learn social skills.
3 As **far** / much as I'm concerned, it's more important to get a good job.
4 **Personally** / Personal, I think that most students work very hard.
5 In my mean / **view**, students need practical skills as well as academic skills.

**8** Match the paragraphs of an opinion essay (1–4) with the functions (a–d).

1 Introduction  ___     3 Argument 2  ___
2 Argument 1    ___     4 Conclusion  ___

a Give another reason to support your opinion with examples.
b Introduce the topic and give your opinion.
c Give a summary of your reasons and give your opinion again in different words.
d Give one reason to support your opinion with examples.

## PLAN

**9** You are going to write an opinion essay with the title: 'Exams are not the best way to test a student's ability.' Use the paragraphs in Exercise 8 and make notes.

## WRITE

**10** Write your opinion essay. Look at page 39 of the Student's Book to help you.

_____
_____
_____
_____
_____
_____
_____
_____
_____
_____
_____
_____
_____
_____
_____
_____
_____

## CHECK

**11** Check your writing. Can you say YES to these questions?

- Have you used the essay structure in Exercise 8?
- Have you used linking phrases to make your essay clearer?
- Have you used the correct quantifiers to make general statements?
- Have you used the correct verb forms in lists with *and* or *or*?
- Have you used different expressions to give your personal opinion?
- Are the spelling and punctuation correct?

**Do you need to write a second draft?**

## Vocabulary
### Training and qualifications

**1** (Circle) **the correct options.**

1 I met my best friend at university. We were studying the same (degree) / career path.

2 To get my qualification, I had to do some **part-time job / work experience** in a big hotel.

3 She couldn't do the course because she couldn't afford the **university degree / course fees**.

4 Before you can go to that school you have to pass an **entrance exam / application form**.

5 Your **career path / training course** has been very unusual – you've had many different jobs.

6 When he was at college, he got a **course fees / part-time job** in a bookshop.

Total: 5

### Achievements

**2 Complete the texts with the phrases in the box. There are two extra phrases.**

> a fortune   a project   ~~a business~~   the community
> awards   a millionaire   record   voluntary work

> Lots of people start ¹_____*a business*_____ but not many of them manage to make ²_____ . The English computer programmer Nick d'Aloisio did both. He created Summly, an app to summarise text, when he was 15, and started his own Internet company. In 2013, at the age of 18, he sold the company to Yahoo for $30m and became ³_____ .

> Malala Yousafzai is a Pakistani teenager who believes girls should have the same opportunities for education as boys. In her town she fought for girls to have support in ⁴_____ so that they could continue their education. Malala has spoken at the United Nations and has been involved in developing ⁵_____ to increase girls' education all over the world. She has won several ⁶_____ , including the Nobel Peace Prize.

Total: 5

## Language focus
### *be going to* and present tenses for the future

**3 Complete the conversations with the correct future form of the verb in brackets.**

1 'Have you got any plans for the summer?'
'Yes, I *'m going to spend* _____ (spend) July with my cousins.'

2 'Is the awards ceremony on TV tonight?'
'Yes, it _____ (start) at 7pm.'

3 'What time _____ (his train/ get) here?'
'It _____ (arrive) at 7 o'clock.'

4 'Is it true? _____ (you/go) for a job interview today?'
'Yes, I _____ (try) to earn some money before university.'

Total: 5

### Predictions with *be going to, will* and *may/might*

**4** (Circle) **the correct options.**

1 She (might) / will win the Nobel Prize but there are lots of other good people.

2 You **'re not going to / might not** break the record today. It's much too windy.

3 I think he **may / will** get a good degree and find a good job. He's a brilliant student.

4 She **might / 's going to** find a part-time job this summer but it isn't easy.

5 They're top and there's only one match left. They **'re going to / may** win the league!

6 I think I **'ll / 'm going to** have a big family.

Total: 5

### Future continuous

**5 Write future continuous sentences with the prompts.**

1 We / break / records / with this project
*We'll be breaking records with this project.*

2 They / not make / a fortune / with that crazy idea!
_____

3 He / star / in Hollywood films / in a year or two
_____

4 She / start / her own company / in a couple of years
_____

5 people / buy / this product / in five years' time?
_____

Total: 4

# Language builder

**6** (Circle) the correct options.

Ainan Cawley was an unusual baby. When he ¹___ eight months old, he ²___ to walk and run, and by one year he ³___ like an adult. By the age of six, he was a chemistry prodigy and from the age of eight he ⁴___ to a university chemistry laboratory several times a week. He also taught ⁵___ biology and how to write computer code. Ainan is now a teenager. He ⁶___ live in Singapore, but now he lives in Malaysia and he ⁷___ to university there since he was eleven. Ainan isn't just a scientist, however. He ⁸___ several film scores, learned to play the piano, and in 2013 he directed his first short film. What will he do next? He ⁹___ become a scientist doing research, or he could choose a career in the arts. One thing is sure, though: Ainan ¹⁰___ to surprise us for many years to come!

| | | | | | | |
|---|---|---|---|---|---|---|
| 1 | a | had been | **(b)** | was | c | has been |
| 2 | a | had learned | b | has learned | c | is learning |
| 3 | a | has talked | b | was talking | c | had talked |
| 4 | a | go | b | used to be | c | would go |
| 5 | a | himself | b | each other | c | yourself |
| 6 | a | had | b | would | c | used to |
| 7 | a | has been going | b | is going | c | went |
| 8 | a | is composing | b | has composed | c | has been composing |
| 9 | a | might | b | will | c | going to |
| 10 | a | continues | b | may continue | c | will be continuing |

Total: 9

# Vocabulary builder

**7** (Circle) the correct options.

1 This charity is trying to ___ young people with no work in the community.
   a develop   **(b)** support   c make
2 I'm really excited ___ getting this award.
   a about   b for   c with
3 When is the entrance ___ for the college?
   a form   b exam   c fees
4 People said I was too young to ___ a company, but they were wrong.
   a bring together   b sign up   c set up
5 I think she'll probably ___ a millionaire with this invention.
   a make   b become   c win
6 It was difficult but I was determined to do ___ .
   a a mistake   b a fortune   c the right thing
7 I didn't ___ him because he got so impatient.
   a happy with   b get on with   c come back
8 It's ___ to find out how many young achievers there are!
   a terrified   b excited   c interesting

Total: 7

# Speaking

**8** (Circle) the correct phrases to complete the conversation.

**Mark:** ¹(We need to decide)/ I'd rather how to choose this year's Student of the Year.
**Will:** Yes, I ²was thinking of / think the best way is to ask everyone to suggest other students.
**Mark:** OK, but that might take a long time.
**Will:** ³How shall we decide / What kind of thing, then?
**Mark:** Well, ⁴that's a good idea / I was thinking of suggesting a category for this year's award. What do you think?
**Will:** OK, ⁵what kind of thing / how shall we decide do you suggest?
**Mark:** Maybe it could be students who've collected money for charity.
**Will:** I don't know. Personally, ⁶I'd rather / we need to decide focus on people who do a lot of voluntary work.
**Mark:** Yes, ⁷that's a good idea / I think the best way is, too.

Total: 6

Total: 46

# Get it right! Unit 3

## *be going to* for the future

Remember that:
- we use **subject + the present tense of *be* + *going to* + infinitive** to talk about future plans and intentions. Remember to use the correct form of *be* and the infinitive.
  - ✓ *I'm going to start driving lessons as soon as I can!*
  - ✗ *I going to start driving lessons as soon as I can!*
  - ✗ *I'm going to starting driving lessons as soon as I can!*
  - ✗ *I'm going to started driving lessons as soon as I can!*
- we use **the present tense of *be* + subject** after question words, e.g. *why, what, when, where, how*.
  - ✓ *What are you going to buy?*
  - ✗ *What you are going to buy?*

### 1 Circle the correct option.
1 What film **we are / are we / we** going to see this afternoon?
2 I'm going to **get / getting / got** a good job after school.
3 They **are going / going / is going** to go to university next year.
4 What **you are / are you / you** going to do when you finish school?
5 My best friend, Amy, is going to **study / studied / studying** History at university.
6 We are going to **spent / spending / spend** the summer holidays in Miami.
7 Where **is he / he is / he** going to meet his sister?
8 He is going to **travelled / travel / travelling** before he goes to university.

## Predictions with *will*

Remember that:
- we use ***will* + infinitive** to make a general prediction or to give an opinion about the future.
  - ✓ *I think you will like my new car when you see it.*
  - ✗ *I think you like my new car when you see it.*
- we make predictions with ***will/won't*** when we feel sure about a future action or event.

### 2 Write sentences about the future with *will*. Use the words given and *will*.
1 I / think / my country / be / different / in 20 years
   *I think my country will be different in 20 years.*
2 My brother / be / successful / in the future
   _____
3 I'm sure / you / enjoy / your new job
   _____
4 If it / rains, / we / have lunch / at my house
   _____
5 They / meet / us / at the station / at 4 o'clock
   _____
6 I / promise / you / that you / not forget / your visit
   _____

## Confusing words: *job, work, career, course*

Remember that:
- we use ***job*** to talk about the regular work that a person does to earn money.
  - ✓ *It's a good idea to get a part-time job.*
  - ✗ *It's a good idea to get a part-time work.*
- we use ***work*** to talk about the activity that someone does in their job.
  - ✓ *His boss thanked him for all his hard work.*
  - ✗ *His boss thanked him for all his hard job.*
- we use ***career*** to talk about a job or series of similar jobs that you do during your working life.
  - ✓ *It's an interesting career and well-paid.*
  - ✗ *It's an interesting course and well-paid.*
- we use ***course*** to talk about a set of lessons or a plan of study on a particular subject, usually leading to an exam or qualification.
  - ✓ *I want to get a job after I finish my course.*
  - ✗ *I want to get a job after I finish my career.*

### 3 Complete the sentences with the correct word – *job, work, course,* or *career*.
1 My mum goes to ___work___ from Monday to Thursday.
2 You should go swimming or play tennis after _____ .
3 If you study hard, you will be able to get a good _____ when you leave school.
4 I'm going to start a _____ in Business English because I want to work in England.
5 She wants to find a new _____ as a doctor in the USA.
6 She worked hard in her _____ and had a great _____ .

# 4 Fabulous food

## Vocabulary

### Cooking verbs

**1** ⭐ **Put the letters in order to make ten cooking verbs.**

| | | | | |
|---|---|---|---|---|
| **1** | pcoh | _chop_ | **6** taros | _____ |
| **2** | sadrep | _____ | **7** ligrl | _____ |
| **3** | ryf | _____ | **8** imx | _____ |
| **4** | bilo | _____ | **9** keab | _____ |
| **5** | selic | _____ | **10** tager | _____ |

**2** ⭐ **Look at the photos and complete the sentences.**

**1** My grandfather ___slices___ his ___bread___ really thin, it's amazing.
**2** It doesn't take long to _____ a strawberry _____ .
**3** How can you _____ _____ without crying?
**4** My mum always _____ _____ for Sunday lunch.
**5** I can't cook much but I can _____ things like _____ .
**6** I usually _____ butter and _____ on my toast.
**7** It's easy to _____ _____ and tomato to make a toasted sandwich.
**8** My mum _____ _____ for exactly 3½ minutes.
**9** We sometimes _____ _____ with honey and nuts to have for dessert.
**10** When I make cakes, I _____ _____ into the mixture.

**3** ⭐⭐ **Complete the recipes with words from Exercise 1. You can use the words more than once.**

**Easy pizza recipe**

First, [1]___spread___ the tomato sauce thickly over the pizza base. [2]_____ the onions, red pepper and mushrooms thinly. Then, [3]_____ the onion and tomato rings over the tomato sauce. Finally, [4]_____ the cheese, and put it over the vegetables. [5]_____ the pizza in the oven for 10–15 minutes.

**Potato salad**

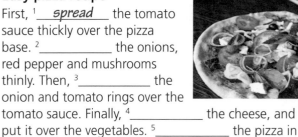

[6]_____ the potatoes, carrots and peas until cooked, and the eggs in a separate pan. When cool, [7]_____ the potatoes, carrots and eggs into small pieces. Finally, [8]_____ all the ingredients together with mayonnaise, salt and pepper.

**Macaroni cheese bake**

First, [9]_____ the macaroni in salty water, then put it in a frying pan with lots of tomato sauce. Then, [10]_____ the macaroni for a few minutes in the pan. Then, put it in a dish, grate or slice some cheese and [11]_____ it over the top. Finally, [12]_____ it in the oven or [13]_____ it until the cheese turns golden brown.

**4** ⭐⭐⭐ **Write about your favourite dish and how to cook it.**

My favourite dish is _____ .
To make it, you'll need _____
_____ .
First, _____
_____ .
Then, _____
_____ .
Finally, _____
_____ .

*My favourite dish is chicken risotto. To make it, you'll need rice, chopped cooked chicken, chopped onion, …*

# Language focus 1

## First conditional with *if*, *when* and *unless*

**1** ★★ **Complete the first conditional sentences with *if*, *when* or *unless*.**

1 Mum, will you get me some crisps ____when____ you go to the supermarket? Thanks!

2 _____ anyone is a vegetarian, I'll buy pepperoni pizzas.

3 I might buy some frozen peas _____ there aren't any green beans.

4 _____ you eat your vegetables, you won't have any dessert.

5 _____ Dad gets home, he'll put the macaroni cheese in the oven. He won't be long.

6 Will you grill the steak _____ I make the salad?

**2** ★★ **Write first conditional sentences with the prompts.**

1 When / they / bring / the ingredients / I / make / the cake
*When they bring the ingredients, I'll make the cake.*

2 The chips / burn / unless / you / fry / them gently
_____

3 If / Paula / cook / tonight / she / make / spaghetti / again
_____

4 you / help / me / with the recipe / when / I / cook supper / tonight?
_____

5 Unless / they / remember / to buy / more bread / we / not have / enough
_____

6 If / he / slice / the tomatoes / with that knife / he / cut / his finger
_____

**3** ★★ Circle **the correct options to complete the mini-conversations.**

**Waiter:** The menu's in Spanish, so I ¹explain / I'll explain if there's anything you ²don't understand / won't understand.

**Jane:** Thanks, but we're fine.

**Ruth:** Sorry, we haven't decided yet.

**Waiter:** That's OK. No hurry. I'll come back ³when / if you're ready to order.

**Ruth:** Mmm. Those mussels look delicious.

**Jane:** But aren't you allergic to shellfish? You ⁴'re / might be really sick if you ⁵eat / 'll eat them.

**Ruth:** ⁶When / Unless I finish this, I ⁷ask / 'll ask for the dessert menu, I think.

**Jane:** I don't know how you can eat so much!

**Jane:** ⁸If / Unless the waiter ⁹brings / will bring the bill soon, we'll be late for the cinema.

**Ruth:** Stop worrying. Here he comes.

**4** ★★★ **Complete the text with *if*, *when* and *unless* and the correct form of the verbs in brackets.**

There's a lot of advice on the Internet about what food is good or bad for you. Things like:

'If you ¹____eat____ (eat) too many eggs, you ²_____ (have) high cholesterol.' 'You ³_____ (not get) heart problems ⁴_____ you eat a low-fat diet.' 'If you ⁵_____ (eat) a lot of garlic, it ⁶_____ (protect) you from illness.' 'You'll put on weight ⁷_____ you eat lots of fruit and vegetables.' 'If your food ⁸_____ (contain) a lot of sugar, you'll develop diabetes.'

But ⁹_____ you actually check these claims, you ¹⁰_____ (find) that they're not completely true. In fact ¹¹_____ you look carefully at the evidence, you'll realise that it's much more complicated than that. So stop worrying. If you eat a good, balanced diet, you ¹²_____ (not have) any problems.

**5** ★★★ **Complete the sentences for you.**

1 When I start living on my own, I won't be able to
_____ .

2 I'll make my own breakfast on Sunday unless ____
_____ .

3 If I go to a restaurant for my next birthday, _____
_____ .

4 _____
_____ if I have to cook this weekend.

5 When I'm older and do all my own cooking, I might _____ .

*When I start living on my own, I won't be able to make very many dishes.*

# Listening and vocabulary

## Adjectives describing food

**1** ★ **Complete the definitions with adjectives describing food.**

**1** Something _salty_ has a lot of salt in it.

**2** Something _____ tastes very good.

**3** Something _____ has salt not sugar in it.

**4** Something _____ isn't sweet.

**5** Something _____ has a lot of sugar in it.

**6** Something _____ doesn't taste good.

**7** Something _____ makes a noise when you eat it.

**8** Something _____ doesn't taste of anything.

**9** Something _____ is soft and oily and not nice.

**10** Something _____ tastes hot when you eat it.

**2** ★★ (Circle) **the correct words.**

**1** You said you could cook! This chicken is (disgusting) / savoury. I can't eat it.

**2** I hate sardines. It's the texture, not the taste, they're really **slimy / bitter**.

**3** Little children usually like **salty / bland** food, without a strong taste.

**4** I prefer **sweet / savoury** snacks, like nuts and crisps, rather than **sweet / savoury** ones, like chocolate bars.

**5** My sister is a really good cook. Everything she makes is **slimy / delicious**.

**6** It's hard to eat crisps secretly. They're so **spicy / crunchy** everyone can hear you!

**7** I don't like dark chocolate. It has a **bitter / delicious** taste. I prefer milk chocolate.

**8** This omelette is really **sweet / salty**. Why did you put so much salt in?

## Listening

**3** ★ 🔊 04 **Listen to a radio programme. What exactly did the man eat recently?**

**4** ★★ 🔊 04 **Listen again and complete the sentences.**

**1** Matt Sanchez makes hot _barbecue sauces_ .

**2** Matt has been visiting the Fiery Foods Festival for _____ .

**3** All the products there are flavoured with _____ .

**4** Chilli peppers first grew in _____ , where children eat hot food and _____ .

**5** Wilbur Scoville invented a way to work out _____ .

**6** The hottest chillies are _____ Scoville units.

**7** The competition involved eating _____ Carolina Reapers in the _____ possible.

**8** Eating _____ or boiled _____ or drinking _____ first can help.

**9** The winner took _____ to eat the Reapers.

**10** The best thing to eat when your mouth is burning is _____ .

# Language focus 2

## Second conditional with *could* and *might*

**1** ⭐ Circle the correct words in the table.

| | |
|---|---|
| **1** | Use the second conditional to talk about situations that are **real / imaginary**. |
| **2** | To form the second conditional, use *if* + the **present simple / past simple** for the situation, and *would, could* or *might / will* or *won't* for a possible consequence. |
| **3** | To form questions, use (question word) + *would / will* + subject + verb. |
| **4** | *If* **can / can't** come at the beginning or in the middle of the sentence/question. |

**2** ⭐ Match the sentence beginnings (1–6) with the sentence endings (a–f).

1 I couldn't work in a restaurant _____*b*_____

2 If you gave up fizzy drinks, _____

3 If you could eat anything now, _____

4 My sister would eat crisps for breakfast _____

5 We could make a cake _____

6 I wouldn't eat broccoli _____

a what would it be?

b if I tried. It's a horrible job.

c if we had some flour.

d unless someone made me.

e you might feel much healthier.

f if my mum didn't stop her.

**3** ⭐⭐ Complete the second conditional sentences. Use the modal verbs in brackets.

1 I can't buy everyone an ice cream because I haven't got enough money. (would)

I _____*would buy*_____ everyone an ice cream if

I _____*had*_____ enough money.

2 I'm not very hungry. That's why I maybe won't eat anything. (might)

If I _____ hungry,

I _____ something.

3 She doesn't know how to cook, so she isn't able to make lunch. (might)

If she _____ how to cook,

she _____ lunch.

4 He doesn't eat goat's cheese because he has a choice. (would)

He _____ goat's cheese unless he _____ no choice.

5 There isn't a pizza delivery service here, so we can't order one. (could)

If _____ a pizza delivery service,

we _____ one.

**4** ⭐⭐⭐ Complete the text with the words in the box. There are two you don't need to use.

| could ask   asked   might be   ~~was/were~~ |
|---|
| wouldn't be   would do   did   would have |
| could discover   would like   wouldn't like |
| prepared   stopped   would stop |

If I [1] _____*was/were*_____ the head teacher of
my school, I [2] _____ something
about school dinners. I [3] _____ my
mum to give the cooks some advice. I'm sure if I
[4] _____ her, she [5] _____
lots of good ideas. I know, some students
[6] _____ happy if the cooks
[7] _____ serving chips with everything,
like they do now, but it [8] _____ healthier
to do that. I also think people [9] _____
it if the cooks [10] _____ food from
a different country or culture once a week.
If they [11] _____ this, everyone
[12] _____ great new foods and recipes.

## Explore prepositional phrases

**5** ⭐ Complete the phrases with the prepositions in the box.

| on ~~(x2)~~   in   by |
|---|

1 _____*on*_____ the streets

2 _____ many different ways

3 surrounded _____

4 _____ the go

**6** ⭐⭐ Complete the sentences with the phrases in Exercise 5.

1 _____*On the streets*_____ of Amsterdam you can buy chips with mayonnaise, spicy croquettes or herrings.

2 I never get bored with potatoes. You can cook them _____ .

3 When I'm _____ , my favourite street food is falafel.

4 My idea of paradise is to be _____ chocolate.

# Reading

**1** ⭐ **Read the article about food in space. Is it still very different from food on Earth?**

## WHAT'S ON THE SPACE MENU TODAY?

Space food used to be boring. Astronauts ate food in bland powders and small cubes, and drank thick liquids from metal tubes. It was like science fiction. If you go into space nowadays, though, you'll eat lots of real food. The International Space Station, or ISS, has astronauts from the USA, Russia, Canada, Europe, China and Japan, who all like different things and eat three meals a day in a personalised menu which repeats every eight days. Each person selects their food in tasting sessions before they go into space, and nowadays there are a wide variety of *tasty* meals and snacks to choose from. The astronauts can choose from pasta or rice, fruit, vegetables, cereal, soup, meat, seafood, yoghurt, nuts, biscuits and more. Drinks include coffee, teas and fruit juice, but no fizzy drinks.

Space food comes in *disposable* packages, and how much preparation it needs on the space station depends on the kind of food. Some foods, like biscuits and fruit, can be eaten out of the packet. Others, such as scrambled eggs, macaroni cheese or rice, are mixed with water, and some, like meat, need to be heated up. There's an oven on the space station to bake things, but there's no fridge, so the food must be carefully prepared and vacuum-packed on Earth so that it will stay fresh.

One strange effect of the microgravity in space is that astronauts have a reduced sense of taste, so all food tastes blander than it would on Earth. For that reason, salty or spicy *seasoning* is really important. Astronauts use a lot of sauces, like chilli pepper sauce, soy sauce, ketchup, mayonnaise and mustard. Salt and pepper are available too, but only in liquid form. If astronauts *sprinkled* salt and pepper on their food in space like we do on Earth, it would just *float away*, and it could damage equipment or get stuck in an astronaut's eyes or nose. Although eating in space nowadays isn't quite like science fiction, it's still not easy!

**2** ⭐ **Complete the definitions with the correct form of the words in bold from the text.**

1 We usually use _____ things once and then throw them away.
2 Food which is _____ is really good to eat.
3 When something moves easily up through the air, like a balloon, it _____ .
4 Salt, pepper, spices and herbs are different kinds of _____ .
5 When we _____ seasoning on food, we gently drop powder or liquid over it.

**3** ⭐⭐ **Read the article again and answer the questions.**

1 Why did food in space use to be like science fiction?
   *Because it was all in powders, small cubes and metal tubes.*
2 Why does each astronaut have their own personalised menu?
   _____
3 Why do they have tasting sessions?
   _____
4 Why is seasoning important in space?
   _____
5 Why is salt and pepper on the space station liquid?
   _____

**4** ⭐⭐ **Complete the information for new astronauts with the words in the box.**

first day   eight   with water   fridge
~~three meals~~   heated up   stays fresh
of the packet   packaging   on Earth   drinks (x2)

## ISS FOOD FACT FILE

Menus: ¹____*Three meals*____ a day + snacks for ²_____ days.

Then menu goes back to the ³_____ .

Choose your menus ⁴_____ .

You will also need to choose ⁵_____ to go with the food.

All food comes in disposable ⁶_____ so it ⁷_____ .

Food may be eaten out ⁸_____ or mixed ⁹_____ or ¹⁰_____ .

On the ISS there are no fizzy ¹¹_____ , and there is no ¹²_____ .

**5** ⭐⭐⭐ **What do you think the biggest problems with food would be for astronauts who had to live in space for several months? What three foods couldn't you live without if you were an astronaut? Write at least five sentences.**

# Writing

## Describing a local dish

**1** Read the description of a local dish. What's the connection between the dish in the picture and the weather in Ireland?

I'm from Ireland and there are two things we love: potatoes and lamb. We eat lots of potatoes and there are lots of sheep in Ireland, so Irish stew is one of our favourite dishes. A stew ¹ ___consists___ of meat and vegetables which are cooked together slowly in a tasty sauce. Irish stew ² _____ lamb, potatoes, carrots and onions. It has everything, but it is often ³ _____ with thick slices of brown bread spread with lots of butter.

Nobody knows who first made Irish stew but because the weather in Ireland is cold and wet, people usually eat a stew on a cold, rainy day. Traditional Irish cooking has many different kinds of stews – with beef, lamb, sausages or fish. People used to make stew over a fire but now it's easier to make on a cooker!

Irish stew is ⁴ _____ in pubs and restaurants all around Ireland, and it's not just for tourists! If you ever go to Ireland, it will probably rain, so try Irish stew for lunch to keep you warm.

**2** Read the description again. Answer the questions.

1 Which two ingredients in Irish stew do Irish people particularly like?
*They like potatoes and lamb.*

2 What are the other ingredients of Irish stew?
_____

3 Who invented Irish stew?
_____

4 What other ingredients might you find in stews in Ireland?
_____

5 How did they make Irish stew in the past?
_____

6 Where can you eat it?
_____

**Useful language** Cooking and eating

**3** Complete the description with the words in the box.

> served ~~consists~~ contains made

**4** Match the sentence beginnings (1–6) with the sentence endings (a–f).

1 Paella is a Spanish dish which consists _____b_____
2 Chicken nuggets contain _____
3 A calzone is pizza bread filled _____
4 Traditional fish and chips are made _____
5 Meat and fish are usually served _____
6 A pie is a pastry dish with fruit or meat baked ___

a in a chip shop or 'chippy'.
b of rice with seafood and meat.
c in an oven.
d with ham, mushrooms and cheese.
e parts of a chicken you wouldn't normally eat.
f with potatoes in Ireland.

**5** Complete the sentences with the correct form of the verb *be*.

1 These dishes _____are_____ served only in the most expensive restaurants in the world.
2 The stew can _____ cooked over a fire.
3 The meat _____ fried before we mix in the vegetables.
4 The cake _____ baked for 30 minutes and then we took it out.
5 Some snacks _____ served in the hotel garden before we sat down to lunch.

# Writing

> **WRITING TIP**
>
> Make it better! ✓ ✓ ✓
> We only use *used to* for <u>past</u> habits. For present
> habits, we use the present simple with *usually*.
> I **used to** *eat a lot of fish when I was younger.*
> I **usually** *go out for dinner with my family on
> special occasions.*

**6** (Circle) **the correct options.**

1 In the past, people (used to)/ usually eat a lot
less sugar.

2 Athletes **used to / usually** have a very strict diet
nowadays.

3 Traditionally, bread **used to / usually** be baked
once or twice a week.

4 My dad **used to / usually** have two cups of
coffee in the morning but not anymore.

5 I **used to / usually** eat fish two or three times
a week. I really like it!

> **WRITING TIP**
>
> Make it better! ✓ ✓ ✓
> End your description with a recommendation for
> the reader.
> *It's a wonderful idea to try local food when you
> travel to new places.*

**7 Read the sentences. Which one is the
strongest recommendation?**

1 If you ever go to Dublin, you should try a full Irish
breakfast.

2 I suggest you try it with a nice salad.

3 Why not go to a local restaurant and try a typical
fish dish?

4 You could have this dish the next time you're in
Istanbul.

5 This dish is absolutely delicious with rice –
you really have to try it!

**8 Look back at the description in Exercise 1.
Complete the plan with the phrases in the box.**

> a recommendation
> ~~the name of the dish~~
> how people cooked the dish in the past
> who invented it
> how to cook the dish
> where you can eat or buy it
> what the ingredients are
> why it's so popular

Paragraph 1 ¹*the name of the dish*
2 _____
3 _____

Paragraph 2 ⁴_____
5 _____
6 _____

Paragraph 3 ⁷_____
8 _____

## PLAN

**9 Think about a traditional dish from another
country that you like. Use the plan in
Exercise 8 and make notes.**

## WRITE

**10 Write a description of the dish. Look at
page 49 of the Student's Book to help you.**

_____
_____
_____
_____
_____
_____
_____
_____
_____
_____
_____
_____
_____
_____
_____
_____
_____
_____

## CHECK

**11 Check your writing. Can you say YES to these
questions?**

• Have you used the ideas in Exercise 8?

• Have you used the phrases for cooking and eating
in Exercise 3?

• Have you used the correct form of *be* in the
phrases?

• Have you used *used to* and *usually* correctly?

• Have you finished the description with a
recommendation?

• Are the spelling and punctuation correct?

**Do you need to write a second draft?**

# Vocabulary
## Cooking verbs

**1 Cross out the word in each sentence which is <u>not</u> correct.**

1 How do you like your eggs? Shall I **fry / boil / ~~grill~~** them?

2 First, **chop / mix / slice** the onions with a sharp knife.

3 I think we should **grate / bake / grill** the fish. It's healthier than frying.

4 **Fry / Boil / Roast** the meat with a little oil.

5 We need to **spread / chop / grate** the cheese all over the pizza.

6 The recipe says we must **boil / bake / roast** it in the oven until it's golden brown.

7 **Spread / Mix / Slice** the mixture with a spoon.

8 Can you **slice / grate / spread** the carrots to put in the salad?

Total: 7

## Adjectives describing food

**2 Complete the sentences with the words in the box.**

> savoury  disgusting  bland  spicy  crunchy
> ~~salty~~  delicious  slimy  bitter  sweet

1 Some seafood is very ___*salty*___ . I suppose it's because of the seawater!

2 They don't like honey. It's too _____ for them.

3 The food at that restaurant was _____ . I want my money back!

4 Little children prefer _____ food which hasn't got a strong taste.

5 Raw fish and oysters are very _____ , but they taste good!

6 I don't like sweet things like cakes and desserts, I prefer _____ food.

7 Mmmm, this cake is really _____ ! Can you give me the recipe?

8 It's difficult to eat _____ food like crisps quietly.

9 You didn't put any sugar in this. It tastes really _____ .

10 In India and Mexico the food is very _____ .

Total: 9

# Language focus
## First conditional with *if*, *when* and *unless*

**3 Write first conditional sentences with *if*, *when* or *unless* and the prompts.**

1 ___ / you / organise the drinks / we / get / the savoury snacks
*If you organise the drinks, we'll get the savoury snacks.*

2 ___ / you / want / to do it yourself / I / make / the birthday cake
_____

3 I / put / the food in the oven / ___ / your friends / arrive / for the party
_____

4 What a big pizza! You / not be able to / eat it all / ___ / I / help / you!
_____

5 Don't worry! I / ring / you / ___ / I / get / home from the restaurant
_____

6 ___ / she / eat / any more crisps / she / might / not want / any supper
_____

Total: 5

## Second conditional with *could* and *might*

**4 Circle the correct options in the text.**

I [1] **would do / did** a cooking course if I [2] **might have / had** enough money. I've thought about it a lot. If I [3] **needed / wouldn't need** to practise, I [4] **cooked / could cook** for my friends and family. Then I [5] **'d feel / felt** more confident as a cook – unless you [6] **wouldn't like / didn't like** my cooking of course, but I can't imagine that! Then, if I [7] **could pass / passed** the course, I [8] **'d look / looked** for a job in a good restaurant. If that [9] **could go / went** well, I [10] **might open / opened** my own restaurant. If I [11] **would own / owned** a restaurant, I [12] **could get / got** a Michelin star one day – why not? And if I [13] **would become / became** a famous chef, I [14] **would appear / appeared** on TV and travel around the world. But I [15] **couldn't do / didn't do** any of this unless I [16] **might have / had** the money for the cooking course. So, can you lend me the money?

Total: 15

## Language builder

**5** Circle the correct options.

| | |
|---|---|
| **Presenter:** | Jimmy, is it true that you and Daniel taught ¹___ to cook? |
| **Jimmy:** | Not really, we went to cookery college! We ²___ share a house with some other students and spend hours in the kitchen! |
| **Presenter:** | And ³___ have you been managing restaurants together? |
| **Jimmy:** | ⁴___ about fifteen years. |
| **Presenter:** | How many restaurants ⁵___ in that time? |
| **Jimmy:** | Six, so far. We ⁶___ our seventh restaurant in the next few months if everything goes well. |
| **Presenter:** | If you had the chance, ⁷___ start a restaurant abroad? |
| **Jimmy:** | Actually, Daniel ⁸___ at some restaurants in New York next month. So I think we ⁹___ our first restaurant in the USA quite soon! |
| **Presenter:** | ¹⁰___ to stop expanding one day? |
| **Jimmy:** | Well, if we want to maintain our quality, we ¹¹___ need to keep the business small. So ¹²___ we put a limit on new restaurants, it will be very difficult to visit them all regularly. |

| | | | | | |
|---|---|---|---|---|---|
| **1** | a yourself | b himself | **c** yourselves | | |
| **2** | a would | b used to | c was | | |
| **3** | a where | b how many | c how long | | |
| **4** | a Since | b For | c Already | | |
| **5** | a have you been opening | b have you opened | c had you opened | | |
| **6** | a will be opening | b won't open | c are opening | | |
| **7** | a will you | b would you | c are you going to | | |
| **8** | a is going to look | b would look | c looks | | |
| **9** | a might open | b won't open | c would open | | |
| **10** | a Will you | b Are you going | c Will you be going | | |
| **11** | a would | b could | c will | | |
| **12** | a unless | b if | c when | | |

Total: 11

## Vocabulary builder

**6** Circle the correct options.

**1** I was really disappointed ___ the new supermarket.
  **a** by  **b** for  **c** at

**2** To become a chef, take a ___ in a cookery school.
  **a** training course  **b** part-time job  **c** work experience

**3** Can you ___ this cheese to put on the pizzas?
  **a** mix  **b** grate  **c** spread

**4** I love the ___ shirt he's wearing. It's so cool!
  **a** flat  **b** leather  **c** denim

**5** If you want to be a top chef, you have to be ___ .
  **a** talented  **b** sociable  **c** easy-going

**6** He has won a lot of ___ for his barbecue sauce.
  **a** fortune  **b** records  **c** awards

**7** If you don't ___ the gas, you'll burn the onions.
  **a** save  **b** turn down  **c** reduce

**8** This chocolate cake mix is too ___ . We need to add more sugar.
  **a** savoury  **b** bitter  **c** sweet

Total: 7

## Speaking

**7** Complete the conversation with the phrases in the box.

> need to stir   finally, when   next, you
> ~~thing to do is~~   first of all, chop   then, add

| | |
|---|---|
| **Nina:** | So, Kate, how do I make the chocolate sauce for the ice cream? |
| **Kate:** | OK, it's easy. The first ¹ _thing to do is_ get all the ingredients ready. |
| **Nina:** | OK, I've got them here. |
| **Kate:** | Great. So, ² _____ the chocolate into small pieces. ³ _____ put them in a bowl over a pan of boiling water. You ⁴ _____ it occasionally. OK? |
| **Nina:** | Yes, I've written that down. Then what? |
| **Kate:** | Put the cream in a saucepan and ⁵ _____ the sugar. Heat it up slowly, and stir it all the time so it doesn't burn. ⁶ _____ the mixture boils, pour it over the chocolate and mix everything together. |

Total: 5

Total: 59

## Second conditional

Remember that:
* we use *if + subject + past simple* in the action/ situation clause.
  ✓ *If you didn't need to study this evening, what would you do instead?*
* we use *would/wouldn't + infinitive* to talk about the consequences. We don't use *will*.
  ✓ *If you didn't need to study this evening, what **would** you **do** instead?*
  ✗ *If you didn't need to study this evening, what ~~will~~ you do instead?*
* we do not use *would/wouldn't + infinitive* in the same clause as *if*.
  ✓ *If you didn't need to study this evening, what would you do instead?*
  ✗ *If you ~~wouldn't need~~ to study this evening, what would you do instead?*
* we form questions with *would(n't) + subject + verb*.
  ✓ *What **would you do** if you didn't need to study?*
  ✗ *What ~~you would~~ do if you didn't need to study?*

**1 Are the sentences correct? Correct the incorrect sentences.**

1 If you would add salt, it tasted better.
   *If you added salt, it would taste better.*

2 What you will cook if you could cook anything you wanted?
   _____

3 It would be nicer if you put grated cheese on it.
   _____

4 The coffee would be less bitter if you would added more sugar to it.
   _____

5 If you would eat a poisonous mushroom, you will be very ill.
   _____

6 Would you eat fugu fish if it will be on the menu?
   _____

## Prepositions: *in* or *on*?

Remember that:
* we use *in* with places like countries, towns and buildings, and with containers.
  ✓ *Fugu fish is a delicacy **in** Japan.*
  ✗ *Fugu fish is a delicacy ~~on~~ Japan.*
* we use *on* with flat or nearly flat surfaces.
  ✓ *What influences the food **on** your plate?*
  ✗ *What influences the food ~~in~~ your plate?*

**2 Complete the sentences with *in* or *on*.**

1 I would order it if it was _____on_____ the menu.
2 They cook food _____ hot rocks _____ this country.
3 We bake our pizzas _____ a special oven.
4 Tourists in Cornwall eat pasties _____ the beach.
5 People _____ Japan live a long time because they eat so much fish.
6 Is there a lot of street food for sale _____ your town?

## Confusing words: *food, meal, dish, plate*

Remember that:
* we use *food* to talk in general about things that people eat to keep them alive.
  ✓ *The most common **food** in Mongolia is meat.*
  ✗ *The most common ~~meal~~ in Mongolia is meat.*
* we use *meal* to talk about an occasion when food is eaten or all the food that is eaten on such an occasion.
  ✓ *At weddings, there is usually a formal **meal**.*
  ✗ *At weddings, there is usually a formal ~~food~~.*
* we use *dish* to talk about food that is served in a particular way as part of a meal.
  ✓ *One of the main **dishes** in my country is pizza.*
  ✗ *One of the main ~~plates~~ in my country is pizza.*
* we use *plate* to talk about a flat, usually round, object that you eat food from or serve food on.
  ✓ *What influences the food on your **plate**?*
  ✗ *What influences the food on your ~~dish~~?*

**3 Circle the correct option.**

1 On the last day of our trip, we had a lovely Arabic food /(meal) in a traditional restaurant.
2 The restaurant offers a variety of delicious traditional plates / dishes to choose from.
3 I like vegetarian meal / dishes like risotto or a cheese omelette.
4 You must try the delicious Greek food / meal in Plaka's famous restaurants.
5 The accommodation includes two foods / meals: breakfast and dinner.
6 I really enjoy eating Japanese meal / food.

# 5 Stuff we like

## Vocabulary
### Everyday objects

**1** ★ **Use the clues to complete the crossword.**

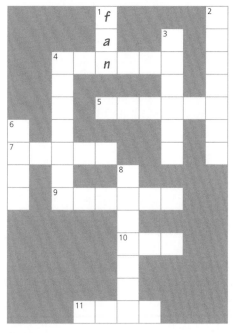

**Across**
4 This gives light without electricity.
5 We use this to turn things on and off.
**7 and 11 across** This helps us to see but it needs electricity. (2 words)
**9 and 8 down** This gives commands to a machine from a distance. (2 words)
10 We get water out of this in the kitchen or bathroom.
11 See 7 across.

**Down**
1 This is useful when it's hot.
2 We use these to light a fire (or light 4 across!).
3 We use this object when it's cold.
4 This gives power to a mobile phone or tablet.
6 This connects a gadget to the electricity supply.
8 See 9 across.

**2** ★★ **Complete the sentences with the correct form of words from Exercise 1.**
1 The _____*plugs*_____ in the USA are different from the ones we have here.
2 The hotel didn't have air conditioning, just big _____ on the ceiling.
3 Where have you put the _____ ? I can't turn on the TV!
4 My sister thinks that _____ are romantic, but I think they're dangerous.
5 Can you help me? I can't turn on the _____ in the bathroom.
6 We need to buy some _____ to light the barbecue. We haven't got any.

**3** ★★ **Complete the leaflet.**

## GET GREEN!

OK. We know you can't buy a TV without a
[1] _*remote control*_ , and your electronic gadgets all have [2]_____ but you can …

⚙ buy low-energy LED [3]_____ – they're cheaper in the end.

⚙ get a special new [4]_____ for the TV and computer, one with a [5]_____ on it so you can turn them off at night.

⚙ put gadgets on the [6]_____ and on the shower so less water comes out.

⚙ wear a jumper if you're cold. Don't put a [7]_____ on instead!

Remember – every little helps!

**4** ★★★ **Write answers to the questions.**
1 Which of the everyday objects do you have in your house? Which room(s) are they in?
2 Do you leave the tap on when you clean your teeth?
3 Do you do any of the things in the leaflet in Exercise 3? Which ones?

*We have lots of chargers, there's one in most rooms in fact.*

# Language focus 1

## The passive: present simple, past simple and *will*

**1** ⭐ **Complete the passive sentences.**

| Active | Passive |
|---|---|
| **Present simple** | |
| They make this tap in gold or silver. | This tap ¹ __*is made*__ in gold or silver. |
| Electric fans don't cool the air. | The air ² _____ by electric fans. |
| **Past simple** | |
| We sold the first microwaves in 1946. | The first microwaves ³ _____ in 1946. |
| Edison didn't invent the light bulb on his own. | The light bulb ⁴ _____ by Edison on his own. |
| ***will*** | |
| They'll show the new range tomorrow. | The new range ⁵ _____ tomorrow. |
| We won't use plugs in the future. | Plugs ⁶ _____ in the future. |

**2** ⭐⭐ **Circle the correct options in the text.**

The first video game, a table tennis game, ¹**invented / was invented** by a physicist in 1958. This ²**followed / was followed** by more sport and space games and the first video arcade game ³**released / was released** in 1971. People ⁴**said / were said** it was too difficult to play! The first Nintendo home consoles ⁵**went / was been** on sale in the 1980s. However, in those days, many games ⁶**played / were played** on PCs. In 1989, the first hand-held console ⁷**saw / was seen** in a few homes. Then in the 1990s PlayStation, still the most popular console, ⁸**developed / was developed**. Nowadays, many teenagers (and adults!) ⁹**spend / are spent** hours playing many different kinds of video games at home, usually on games consoles. Sometimes tournaments ¹⁰**play / are played** on the Internet by people who never meet. I'm not sure what new games ¹¹**will design / will be designed** in the future, but I'm sure teenagers ¹²**will find / will be found** them exciting.

**3** ⭐⭐ **Complete the sentences with the correct active or passive form of the verbs in brackets.**

1 Experts predict that in 20 years' time 20% of shopping __*will be done*__ (do) online.
2 Apparently, low-energy light bulbs _____ (invent) by General Electric in the USA in the 1970s, but they _____ (not manufacture) until the 1980s because they were very expensive.
3 Over a billion mobile phones _____ (sell) worldwide every year, and they all have a charger. I'm sure a lot of these chargers _____ (not need).
4 Centuries ago, people in Africa and the Middle East _____ (not use) candles. They used olive oil lamps instead.
5 In the future, products bought online _____ (not deliver) in a van. Soon robot delivery planes _____ (test) in the USA.
6 The first TV remote control _____ (make) in 1956. It used ultrasonic signals. Nowadays, infrared light _____ (use), which is invisible to the human eye.

**4** ⭐⭐⭐ **Complete the text with the correct passive form of the verbs in the box. Add *by* if necessary.**

> hold  injure  order  finish  fly
> release  add  ~~delay~~  edit  film

| Home | World news | Health news | | Tech news | ▲ |
|---|---|---|---|---|---|
| | | | Film news | | |

Two months ago, the production of the new Jay Jones film ¹ __*was delayed*__ for six weeks when Jay ² _____ in a fall during an action scene and ³ _____ to hospital by helicopter. He'd broken his ankle and ⁴ _____ his doctors to rest for six weeks. The action scenes ⁵ _____ in Botswana.

Now, Jay himself tells us that filming ⁶ _____ at last. However, we have to wait while the film ⁷ _____, and the special effects ⁸ _____.

The film ⁹ _____ Universal next year, and the premiere ¹⁰ _____ in Botswana. We can't wait!

▼

# Listening and vocabulary

## Listening

**1** ★ 🔊 **05** **Listen to Andy talking about his toy collection. Why is he so excited?**

a He has been given more toys.

b He's going to sell his old toys.

**2** ★★ 🔊 **05** **Listen again and choose the correct answers.**

**1** Where is Andy going soon?

ⓐ to college

b to a collector's shop

c to see his friends

**2** What did his mother want him to do?

a clean his toys

b tidy up his toys

c sell his toys

**3** What toys did he collect?

a cars and trucks

b Action Man figures

c toys which change into something else

**4** Who gave him more toys?

a his friends and his uncle

b his family, especially his uncle

c No one. He bought them all.

**5** How many does he have in his collection?

a more than 500

b about 1,000

c several thousand

**6** Which <u>two</u> problems are there with the toys at the moment?

a There are too many for the room.

b They are too old.

c They will get dirty.

**7** What did he find out about his toys on the Internet?

a He can't sell them online.

b Lots of people buy them.

c Only a few people want them.

**8** How much money could he get?

a a thousand dollars

b a few thousand dollars

c seven thousand dollars

## Modifiers

**3** ★ **Which sentence in each pair is stronger?** Circle **a or b.**

**1** a This game is really difficult.

ⓑ This game is ridiculously difficult.

**2** a This light is a bit bright.

b This light is much too bright.

**3** a These toys are totally amazing.

b These toys are kind of amazing.

**4** a Your clothes are quite dirty.

b Your clothes are extremely dirty.

**4** ★★ Circle **the correct words in the text.**

I started collecting Star Wars figures when I was [1] quite / totally young – about six or seven, I think. For a child they were [2] **ridiculously / much** expensive, but I got them as presents from my family, and saved all my pocket money to buy more. For a few years I was [3] **totally / kind** obsessed with them, and my collection grew and grew. My bedroom was [4] **extremely / much** too small for them all, so it was a [5] **really / bit** difficult to tidy up. I was [6] **really / bit** surprised when my dad said I could sell them for $5,000! I was [7] **kind / ridiculously** of sad to see them go, but my parents were [8] **much too / extremely** happy!

# Language focus 2

## Relative pronouns and clauses

**1** ★ **Complete the sentences with the correct relative pronoun. Sometimes two words are possible.**

1 Wasn't she the woman __who/that__ made the perfumed candles?
2 That's the hotel _____ we stayed on holiday last year.
3 Those are the people _____ son is a professional footballer.
4 Is this the bicycle _____ you're selling?
5 He was the teacher _____ helped me to understand Maths.
6 We visited the village _____ my mother was born.
7 I've lost the earrings _____ I got for my birthday.
8 He's the actor _____ daughter is in my class.

**2** ★★ **Write sentences with the prompts. Use relative pronouns.**

1 This / be / the family / I / stay / with / in France
   _This is the family who/that I stayed with in France._
2 This / be / the house / I / stay
   _____
3 That / be / Xavier, / the boy / I / do / the exchange with
   _____
4 That / be / Emil, / the little brother / bedroom / I / share
   _____
5 That / be / Serge, / the brother / Xavier / share a room with
   _____
6 These / be / the pancakes / we / eat / for breakfast / every day
   _____
7 These / be / the neighbours / swimming pool / we / use / while / I / be there
   _____
8 This / be / the café / we / go / to play pool
   _____

**3** ★★ **Join the sentences using a relative pronoun and a relative clause.**

1 She's the woman. I told you about her.
   _She's the woman who/that I told you about._
2 That is the restaurant. We had lunch there.
   _____
3 They are the people. They won the lottery.
   _____
4 She's the neighbour. Her car was stolen.
   _____
5 These are the jeans. I bought them yesterday.
   _____
6 I love the shop. I buy cheap video games there.
   _____
7 Liam is the boy. I sold my old games console to him.
   _____
8 Those are the people. Their cat is missing.
   _____

**4** ★★★ **Choose some photos from a holiday or another event. Write at least five sentences about places, people and things.**

*These are my friends Anni and Dana who I was camping with.*

## Explore communication phrases and phrasal verbs

**5** ★★ **Complete the text with the correct form of the words in the box.**

> keep in touch (x2)   lose touch
> catch up   track down   Tweet
> Skype™   text   chat   email

When my parents went away to university, it was difficult for them to ¹__*keep in touch*__ with their friends from school. There were no computers or Internet, and people had to send letters, they couldn't just ²_____ each other. They didn't have mobile phones, so ³_____ was impossible too, and ⁴_____ on the phone was expensive. So in those days, most people ⁵_____ with the people they went to school with. That's why when Facebook came along, lots of older people used it to ⁶_____ their old friends again, so that they could ⁷_____ with all their news. Young people now can always ⁸_____ with their friends. Apart from Facebook, they can ⁹_____ all their news instantly with Twitter, and by making a ¹⁰_____ video call, they can see each other, too! The world has totally changed!

# Reading

**1** ★ **Read the article about gadgets. Tick (✓) the power source they all use.**

## 2 ★★ Match the words in **bold** in the text with the definitions.

1 liquids can't go through it      _____
2 turn a key or a wheel round and round      _____
3 a metal or plastic circle to keep something in position      _____
4 the part of something you can hold and move      _____
5 doesn't damage the environment      _____

## 3 ★★ Read the first two paragraphs of the article again. Complete the sentences.

1 Clockwork devices lost popularity because of _batteries and electricity_ .
2 Baylis designed the clockwork radio because many people _____ .
3 Some clockwork devices are more sophisticated because they have _____ .
4 Eco-friendly people use clockwork gadgets because they _____ .

## 4 ★★ Read about the gadgets again. What is each sentence about? Write *BL* for the bicycle light, *T* for the torch or *MP* for the media player.

1 This gadget does two different things.    _T_
2 You can charge this in different ways.    ___
3 This runs the longest after one minute of winding.    ___
4 You can do lots of different things with this.    ___
5 This could help you if you have an unexpected problem.    ___
6 This can be put on and taken off something.    ___

## 5 ★★★ Have you got or seen any clockwork gadgets? Would you use any of the gadgets in the article? Which one(s) and why?

# SAY BYE BYE TO BATTERIES

Before watches with batteries were invented in the 1950s, all watches were clockwork – you had to **wind** them every day or they stopped. Clockwork devices had been around for centuries, but when batteries and electricity came along, clockwork was forgotten. Then, in the 1990s, British inventor Trevor Baylis invented a clockwork radio which could be used in parts of Africa where there was no electricity, or where electricity was much too expensive for most people. This quickly became extremely popular throughout Africa and Asia.

Baylis' radio has a **handle** which you turn to charge a generator inside the radio. There are no batteries, but when the generator is fully wound it produces enough electricity to run for 8 hours. On more sophisticated devices, a rechargeable battery is charged when the handle is turned. Baylis designed his products for countries with little or no electricity, but nowadays clockwork gadgets are also used in Europe and America by **eco-friendly** people who want to use less electricity.

## Here are just a few of the gadgets available:

### Bicycle Light

1 minute of winding gives 90 minutes of light, with 1 or 3 LED bulbs. When fully charged, the light works for 5 hours. It comes with a **clamp** to fix easily onto your bike.

### LED Torch

The torch gives 8 hours constant light on full charge – nearly 20 minutes winding. It is designed to be **waterproof** and strong and won't stop working if you drop it. It even has an emergency mobile phone charger and adaptors for all popular phones!

### Eco-friendly Media Player

This is an MP3 Player, ebook reader and photo viewer. The clockwork system means that you won't run out of power or use batteries that harm the environment. 1 minute of winding gives 40 minutes of play time (up to 6 hours fully charged) – great for the beach or camping. It can also be charged normally through your computer.

Thanks to Baylis, clockwork gadgets are saving money, saving energy and saving the planet!

# Writing

## An online review

**1** Read the review of a smartwatch. What can you do with it?

# GEAR REVIEW

### PRODUCT

The new GKQ Smartwatch

### DESIGN

The latest GKQ Smartwatch is ¹____*available in*____ three colours: black, white and, my favourite, 'champagne', which ²_____ really cool.

### PERFORMANCE

The battery can last for up to seven days and the touchscreen is ³_____ a special material which doesn't reflect the sun, so the image is always clear and it's big enough to see a good amount of text. You can send and receive messages and emails, view and update your social media networks and even monitor your heart rate. Of course you ⁴_____ to see what time it is!

### EASE OF USE

The smartwatch is really easy to use – with touchscreen and voice commands. This latest version has a button on the side which makes it easier to change what you see on the screen so you don't have to swipe with your finger. The watch ⁵_____ a rubber strap which you can change if you like.

### EXTRA FEATURES

The GKQ Smartwatch is totally waterproof, so you can wear it in the shower. The case is made of metal, so it's very strong, and you can buy a wireless headset to receive and make calls. The headsets ⁶_____ five different colours.

### OVERALL OPINION

Smartwatches aren't cheap but this one isn't too expensive and the range of functions makes it very attractive.

**2** Read the review again. Are these sentences true or false? Correct the false sentences.

1 The smartwatch comes in red and black. ✗
   *The smartwatch comes in white, black*
   *and 'champagne'.*

2 The battery lasts for more than a week.
   _____

3 You can check your email on it.
   _____

4 You can talk to your smartwatch.
   _____

5 You probably shouldn't wear it in the shower.
   _____

6 It's good value for money.
   _____

**Useful language** Describing a product

**3** Complete the review with the phrases in the box.

> comes with   looks   made of   come in
> ~~available in~~   can also use it

**4** Write sentences with the prompts.

1 The TV / come / three different colours
   *The TV comes in three different colours.*

2 The pink phone / look / very cool
   _____

3 The camera / only / available / black
   _____

4 The screen / made / plastic
   _____

5 You / also use it / make phone calls
   _____

6 The tablet / come / several apps
   _____

> **WRITING TIP**
>
> **Make it better! ✓ ✓ ✓**
> Use relative clauses to give other information in your review.
> *It's really incredible! It's a remote control **which** can control all the gadgets in your home.*
> *The person **who** invented it was obviously a genius!*

# Writing

**5** **Match the sentence beginnings (1–6) with the sentence endings (a–f).**

1 The phone has a metal case ___*f*___
2 The product comes with its own store ___
3 It looks great thanks to the designer, Haruto Saito, ___
4 This is the new phone from the people at CQ ___
5 It comes with headphones ___
6 The camera has a 1TB memory card ___

a whose tablets have been really successful.
b who comes from Japan.
c which means you can take lots of photos.
d that fit nicely in your ears.
e where you can download the apps you want.
f which makes it quite heavy.

**6** **Complete the sentences with *too* or *enough* and the adjectives in brackets.**

1 It's ___*small enough*___ to fit in your pocket. (small)
2 I don't think the screen is _____ , because it's hard to read the text. (big)
3 At €550 I think it's _____ because there are cheaper models. (expensive)
4 Some people say its battery life isn't _____ but I disagree. (long)
5 The box was _____ and it broke when I opened it. (weak)
6 The cable is _____ , which is quite annoying. (short)

> **WRITING TIP**
>
> Make it better! ✓ ✓ ✓
> Use positive language to make your review sound better.
> *The high-definition screen is **absolutely incredible** and the sound quality is **really good** too.*

**7** **Rewrite these sentences to make them sound more positive. Use the words in brackets.**

1 At €150, this phone is cheap. (incredible, really)
   *At €150, this incredible phone is really cheap.*
2 The design looks good. (amazing)
   _____
3 The phone has a large screen. (very)
   _____
4 The remote control is easy to use. (incredibly)
   _____
5 The range of colours is very good. (spectacular)
   _____
6 It's a nice size. (perfect)
   _____

**8** **Read the review in Exercise 1 again and tick (✓) the information it includes.**

name of the product ✓
colours available ☐
functions – what it does ☐
price ☐
personal opinion ☐
comparison with other products ☐
options or accessories ☐
features – special things about it ☐

## PLAN

**9** **Think about a gadget (e.g. a smartphone, a tablet, a camera, etc.) that you would like to buy. Use the categories in Exercise 8 and make notes.**

## WRITE

**10** **Imagine you have bought the gadget. Write a product review for a website. Look at page 61 of the Student's Book to help you.**

_____
_____
_____
_____
_____
_____
_____
_____
_____
_____
_____
_____
_____
_____
_____
_____
_____

## CHECK

**11** **Check your writing. Can you say YES to these questions?**

- Have you used the ideas in Exercise 8?
- Have you used the phrases for describing a product in Exercise 3?
- Have you used relative pronouns correctly?
- Have you used adjectives with *too* and *enough* and checked the word order?
- Have you used positive language to make your review sound better?
- Are the spelling and punctuation correct?

**Do you need to write a second draft?**

## Vocabulary
### Everyday objects

**1** Match the sentences (1–10) with the sentences (a–j) that follow them.

1  I need to borrow a charger. _g_
2  I can't use my laptop plug in Europe. ___
3  I think we should turn on the fan. ___
4  Can you pass me the remote control? ___
5  Where's the switch on the printer? ___
6  This light bulb isn't very bright. ___
7  Why haven't you put the heater on? ___
8  There's only one tap in the kitchen. ___
9  I think that's a beautiful candle. ___
10  Have you got any matches? ___

a  I want to change the channel.
b  It mixes the hot and cold water.
c  It's freezing in here.
d  It's American, so it doesn't work here.
e  We want to light the candles on the cake.
f  When it burns, it smells of roses.
g  My phone battery has died!
h  It's really hot in here.
i  I can't see where it turns on.
j  I can't see what I'm reading.

Total: 9

### Modifiers

**2** Circle the correct options.

1  The first light bulb was **a bit / ridiculously** bright and was no good for everyday use.
2  The heater was **kind of / much too** expensive for me. It cost $200, and I only had $40.
3  I thought the film was **totally / quite** good, but not one of the best I'd seen.
4  It is **extremely / a bit** cold in Siberia in winter, sometimes −50°C.
5  The fan was **a bit / ridiculously** noisy, but not too bad, and without it the room was too hot.
6  You have to be **really / much too** rich to have gold bath taps.
7  The room looked **kind of / ridiculously** mysterious with all the candles lit and the lights off.
8  Most of their possessions were **totally / a bit** destroyed in the fire.

Total: 7

## Language focus
### The passive: present simple, past simple and *will*

**3** Complete the texts using passive forms.

The first luxury scented candles ¹_**were developed**_ (develop) by Mario and Viviane Rigaud of the French perfume house Rigaud in the 1950s. The special soft wax ²_____ (invent) by Mario himself. Nowadays, the Rigaud 'Cyprès' candle ³_____ (sell) all over the world, and there are many other scented candles too.

These days remote controls for TVs and other machines ⁴_____ (find) in every home. Universal remotes ⁵_____ (produce) by several different companies, but they aren't easy to use. However, experts predict that they ⁶_____ (not need) in the future. They say our remotes ⁷_____ (replace) by smartphone apps.

Total: 6

### Relative pronouns and clauses

**4** Write sentences using the prompts and a relative pronoun.

1  That / be / the birthday present / I / buy / for my mum / last weekend
   _That's the birthday present which I bought for my mum last weekend._

2  Xavi / be / the boy / dad / use to / work / with my dad / years ago
   _____

3  Yesterday / we / visit / the museum / Edison's / first light bulbs / be displayed
   _____

4  This / be / the guitar / he / make / himself / at the age of 16!
   _____

5  Is / that / the man / help you / the other day?
   _____

6  I / think / that / be / the girl / bag / you / find / this morning
   _____

Total: 5

# Language builder

**5** (Circle) the correct options.

It's difficult to remember that, when our grandparents were young, they ¹___ have mobile phones or the Internet. Since then, there ²___ so many technological advances. In the year 2000 the first smartphone ³___ , and more recently, several technology companies ⁴___ smart *glasses* you can wear. ⁵___ them in five years' time? They haven't arrived in the shops yet, but the glasses ⁶___ on sale very soon. If you ⁷___ a pair of smart glasses, you will be able to download apps, just like on a smartphone, and the information ⁸___ you ask for ⁹___ on the glass. Amazing!

| | **a** | **b** | **c** | **d** |
|---|---|---|---|---|
| **1** | wouldn't | used to | (c) didn't use to | would |
| **2** | have been | was | had been | were |
| **3** | is produced | produced | was produced | has produced |
| **4** | has developed | had developed | was developing | have been developing |
| **5** | Will we be wearing | Are we wearing | Have we worn | Do we wear |
| **6** | would be | won't be | are | may be |
| **7** | will buy | buy | might buy | bought |
| **8** | whose | who | that | what |
| **9** | displayed | will be displayed | was displayed | display |

Total: 8

# Vocabulary builder

**6** (Circle) the correct options.

1 He's got a university ___ in physics.
   **a** career path   **(b)** degree   **c** work experience

2 Don't leave the ___ on. It wastes water.
   **a** switch   **b** tap   **c** remote control

3 There was a lot of competition to succeed, but he didn't ___ .
   **a** give up   **b** count on   **c** pass on

4 Mmmm. These chips are really ___ . Fantastic!
   **a** crunchy   **b** slimy   **c** bland

5 I need a new ___ for my desk lamp. I can't study at the moment, it's too dark.
   **a** heater   **b** fan   **c** light bulb

6 Her uncle started a ___ selling candles and made a fortune.
   **a** business   **b** project   **c** work

7 That jumper is ___ cheap. The price must be a mistake!
   **a** much   **b** ridiculously   **c** a bit

8 I'm really excited. We're going on a ___ in March.
   **a** summer camp   **b** school exchange
   **c** trekking

9 I don't understand why people get so ___ about technology.
   **a** happy   **b** afraid   **c** excited

10 We ___ the chicken in the oven. It was delicious.
   **a** fried   **b** grilled   **c** roasted

Total: 9

# Speaking

**7** **Complete the conversation with the phrases in the box.**

> ~~Can you tell me about~~   Could you show
> How long does … last   Is it easy
> How much memory   What's … like

**Dave:** Excuse me, ¹ _Can you tell me about_ that tablet over there?

**Assistant:** Yes, of course.

**Dave:** Great … ² _____ to use?

**Assistant:** Yes, very.

**Dave:** Right, and ³ _____ has it got?

**Assistant:** 16GB.

**Dave:** That's good. ⁴ _____ the sound _____ ?

**Assistant:** Oh, quite good for videos and music.

**Dave:** OK. ⁵ _____ the battery _____ ?

**Assistant:** It has 12 hours of screen time.

**Dave:** Right. ⁶ _____ it to me?

Total: 5

Total: 49

## Passive with *will*

Remember that:
- we use *will + be* + past participle to talk about actions we believe will happen in the future.
  - ✓ A prize *will be given* for the best idea.
  - ✗ A prize *will give* for the best idea.
  - ✗ A prize *will given* for the best idea.
  - ✗ A prize *be given* for the best idea.

**1** **Complete the sentences with the passive form of the verb in brackets and *will/won't*.**

1 The programme ____*will be shown*____ (show) on the History Channel tonight at 8 pm.

2 The food _____ (make) by my mother, who is an excellent cook.

3 Millions of pounds _____ (spend) on building the new recycling centre.

4 In the future, videos of the sky _____ (see) on the inside of aeroplane windows.

5 A railway line under the sea _____ (create) between London and New York.

6 More than six hundred passengers _____ (carry) on each train.

**Spell it right!** Past participles

Remember that:
- with irregular verbs, the past simple form of the verb and the past participle are sometimes different and sometimes the same.
  - ✓ A prize will be *given* to the winner.
  - ✓ A prize was *given* to the winner.
  - ✓ This is the birthday present that my brother *gave* me.

**2** **Write the correct past simple and past participle form of these irregular verbs from Unit 5. There is an irregular verb list at the back of the Student's Book.**

| Infinitive | Past simple | Past participle |
|---|---|---|
| give | *gave* | _____ |
| leave | _____ | _____ |
| sell | _____ | _____ |
| make | _____ | _____ |
| find | _____ | _____ |
| show | _____ | _____ |
| see | _____ | _____ |
| spend | _____ | _____ |

## Relative pronouns and clauses

Remember that:
- we use relative pronouns at the beginning of relative clauses to refer to the subject of the main clause. We do <u>not</u> use an object pronoun in the relative clause.
  - ✓ He's an interesting person *who* I like a lot.
  - ✗ He's an interesting person who I like *him* a lot.
- we use *which* or *that* to talk about things. We do not use *what*.
  - ✓ I need something *that* I can put on my desk.
  - ✗ I need something *what* I can put on my desk.

**3** **Are the sentences correct? Correct the incorrect sentences.**

1 The website will tell you all the information ~~what~~ <sub>∧</sub> *that* you need to know.

2 There is a park in the city which it is very clean and quiet.

3 There are a lot of drivers who they do not know how to drive very well.

4 I got the part-time job in London what I wanted!

5 I've moved to a new house which it's a bit bigger.

6 My friend whose dad is a famous actor has invited me to a party.

7 That is the girl who I told you about her.

8 I'm looking for a man who he left his mobile phone in the café.

**Spell it right!** Modifiers

B1 and B2 students often make spelling mistakes when writing these modifiers. Remember to spell them correctly.

| | | |
|---|---|---|
| really | extremely | a bit |
| quite | totally | |

**4** **Find and correct three more spelling mistakes with the modifiers in these sentences.**

1 Matches are a ~~realy~~ <sub>∧</sub> *really* useful thing to take when you go camping.

2 Don't touch the light bulb! It's extremly hot.

3 Mobile phone chargers can be quiet expensive.

4 Our new remote control is a bit easier to use than the old one.

5 The light in a bottle is a totaly unique invention.

# 6 Celebrate in style

## Vocabulary

### Celebrations

**1** ★ **Find seven more verbs in the first wordsquare and seven more nouns in the second.**

verbs

| g | o | p | l | a | y |
|---|---|---|---|---|---|
| i | b | d | o | v | e |
| v | h | r | s | e | t |
| e | a | e | t | h | k |
| m | v | s | w | o | p |
| d | e | s | t | l | u |
| m | a | k | e | d | x |
| s | a | d | p | u | t |

nouns

| s | t | e | p | l | a | d | y | z |
|---|---|---|---|---|---|---|---|---|
| p | i | q | r | o | y | e | n | o |
| i | m | p | e | r | f | c | u | p |
| b | e | n | s | f | m | o | c | h |
| f | i | r | e | w | o | r | k | s |
| i | n | u | n | o | t | a | c | p |
| c | o | n | t | e | s | t | u | f |
| t | u | s | x | b | r | i | j | o |
| o | c | c | a | s | i | o | n | o |
| x | k | r | m | h | s | n | o | d |
| t | m | u | s | i | c | s | h | l |

**2** ★ **Complete the phrases for celebrations with the verbs and nouns in Exercise 1.**

1 ___play___ ___music___
2 _____ special _____
3 _____ a _____
4 _____ off _____
5 _____ a good _____
6 _____ up for the _____
7 _____ up _____
8 _____ a _____

**3** ★★ **Complete the sentences with phrases from Exercise 2.**

1 At the festival in my village, they always ___hold a contest___ to find the best karaoke singer.
2 No! You can't _____ your favourite _____ at the party. It's too slow and no one can dance to it.
3 When it's a friend's birthday, we collect money and _____ them _____ from everyone.
4 I like it when we have a family dinner and my grannies _____ .
5 Before the party, we _____ all round the school hall to make it look good.
6 Her parties are great. We always _____ !

**4** ★★ **Complete the text with the correct form of phrases from Exercise 2.**

August 17ᵗʰ is Independence Day in Indonesia. In preparation, people ¹___put up___ colourful _decorations_ on buildings and in streets all over town. All week, live concerts and TV shows ²_____ popular _____ . On the day itself, there is an official ceremony where school children and the military ³_____ in smart uniforms. There are also local street parties with games and races. Special ⁴_____ is _____ for cooking and eating competitions, especially shrimp crackers. Also, local communities ⁵_____ another popular _____ called _Panjat Pinang_. People try and climb a very greasy palm tree trunk. At the top are prizes like bikes and TVs. Everyone ⁶_____ , especially the people watching the fun! At the end of the day, noisy and spectacular ⁷_____ are _____ – an exciting end to a great celebration.

**5** ★★★ **Think of a different celebration where you live or in another country. What happens at it? Write at least five sentences.**

_At weddings in Turkey, the couple are given gold coins._

# Language focus 1

## -ing forms

### 1 ⭐ Complete the rules in the table.

| | |
|---|---|
| **1** | We use -ing forms as _____ . |
| **2** | We also use -ing forms after _____ . |
| **3** | We also use them after certain _____ and expressions (e.g. like, can't stand). |

### 2 ⭐ Circle the -ing forms in these sentences. Which rule in Exercise 1 matches each sentence?

1 He gets quite nervous before (competing) in a contest.     Rule _2_

2 I love watching fireworks, but the noise sometimes makes me nervous.     Rule ___

3 How shall we celebrate passing our exams?     Rule ___

4 I can't imagine a party that doesn't have music and dancing.     Rule ___

5 I always look forward to putting up the decorations at Christmas.     Rule ___

6 We plan to save money by making the food ourselves.     Rule ___

7 Choosing presents for my dad is quite difficult.     Rule ___

8 In my family, we believe in celebrating everything together.     Rule ___

### 3 ⭐⭐ Write sentences with the prompts. Use -ing forms where necessary.

1 Go / to a prom / can / cost / a lot of money
*Going to a prom can cost a lot of money.*

2 You / can not / organise / a big party / without / have / a few problems
_____

3 My mum / really / enjoy / go / to weddings
_____

4 Wear / special clothes / make / me / feel / uncomfortable
_____

5 You / must / practise / make / a speech / before / the awards ceremony
_____

6 I / not be / very good at / sing / or / dance
_____

7 Some people / can't stand / be / in a large crowd / at a concert
_____

8 The best thing / about / go / to the festival / be / see / the fireworks
_____

### 4 ⭐⭐⭐ Write answers to the questions.

1 What are you looking forward to soon?
_____

2 What do you miss about being at primary school?
_____

3 What do you like doing on your birthday?
_____

4 How do people in your country celebrate leaving school?
_____

5 What's the best thing about being you?
_____

*Next weekend, I'm looking forward to going to a friend's party. It's in a restaurant.*

## Explore verbs and prepositions

### 5 ⭐ Match the verbs and prepositions (1–6) with the definitions (a–f).

1 work with
2 agree on
3 look forward to
4 recover from
5 prepare for
6 arrive at

a return to normal after a difficult time
b get ready for an event
c do a job/project together with someone
d get to a destination
e make a decision about something together
f feel excited about a future event

### 6 ⭐⭐ Complete the email with the correct form of the verbs and prepositions in Exercise 5.

✉ *Your*MAIL    ⊕ New    Reply | ▼    Delete    Junk | ▼

Hi Janey,

I hope you ¹ _arrived at_ your friend's birthday party all right yesterday. It was nice to see you in town. I forgot to say that this year my school is ² _____ two other schools to organise the end-of-year prom. At first, we couldn't ³ _____ a date, but now it's on the last day of term, so we can all ⁴ _____ our exams first. Of course, we've got a lot to do to ⁵ _____ it, but lots of people are helping. It should be fun! I'm really ⁶ _____ it! Does your school have a prom?

Mabel

# Listening and vocabulary

## Listening

**1** ★ 🔊 06 **Listen to the organiser of a music festival explaining her job. Tick (✓) the two areas she talks about.**

festival food ☐   why people camp ☐

cleaning up ☐   booking bands ☐

**2** ★★ 🔊 06 **Listen again. Are these sentences true (*T*) or false (*F*)?**

1 Emma has only just started this job.    *F*

2 Over one hundred thousand people went to the festival this year.    ___

3 Campers have to get rid of their own rubbish after the festival.    ___

4 Many people don't take their tents home with them after the festival.    ___

5 Taking down all the facilities after the festival takes three months.    ___

6 Some of the bands are booked a long time before they play.    ___

7 Emma tells the presenter the names of the headline acts for the next festival.    ___

8 The festival has many different types of music.    ___

9 Emma asks for advice about different acts from record companies.    ___

10 She gets some requests from fans who want to play at the festival.    ___

## Descriptive adjectives

**3** ★ Circle **the correct words.**

1 The classical music was really **scary /** **atmospheric**. Everyone loved it.

2 The square was really **impressive / crowded** because there were too many people watching the fireworks.

3 The bride looked **stunning / colourful** in her simple white wedding dress.

4 Lots of the dancers were dressed like zombies. They were quite **traditional / scary**.

5 Look! The street decorations are really **impressive / peaceful**. Absolutely amazing!

6 Although the festival is very **traditional / atmospheric**, a lot of young people take part.

7 After the big parade had gone by, the streets were **stunning / peaceful** again.

8 The dancers' costumes were so **crowded / colourful**. I took some great pictures.

**4** ★★ **Complete the text with words from Exercise 3.**

This Irish Music festival is held on a farm in a ¹ *stunning* location near a lake. Two weeks before it starts, the fields are still empty and ² _____, with only a few cows. Then the organisers arrive, and it's really ³ _____ that they can get everything ready in such a short time. The gates open on Friday morning and by Friday night the festival is always ⁴ _____ with people and tents. On the big outdoor stage, the rock bands play, with their ⁵ _____ light shows. In the folk tent, the music is more ⁶ _____ , with musicians playing all the old songs as well as new ones, and everyone singing along. With the lake, the sky and the friendly people, the whole scene is quite ⁷ _____ . It's a wonderful festival!

# Language focus 2

## Infinitives

**1** ⋆ **Complete the rules in the table.**

| | |
|---|---|
| **1** | We use infinitives after _____ (e.g. *difficult*, *worst*). |
| **2** | We use infinitives after certain _____ (e.g. *want*, *need*). |

**2** ⋆ (Circle) **the infinitives in these sentences and look at the words before them. Which rule in Exercise 1 matches each sentence?**

1 She hopes (to celebrate) her birthday at the beach.   Rule _2_

2 It's not easy to organise a music festival.   Rule ___

3 It's probably best to practise a few times first!   Rule ___

4 We'd like to go away for New Year.   Rule ___

5 They decided to wear costumes to the celebrations.   Rule ___

6 It's great to be here for this fantastic festival.   Rule ___

**3** ⋆⋆ **Complete the texts with the infinitive form of the verbs in the boxes.**

> visit   go   agree   celebrate   ~~take~~   think

My grandparents have offered ¹__*to take*__ all my family on holiday, so we've decided ²_____ New Year somewhere different this year. It's not easy ³_____ on where to go. I'd like ⁴_____ to New York, but my parents want ⁵_____ Rio. It's just exciting ⁶_____ we're going away – it doesn't matter where!

> have   take   find   tell

I'd hoped ⁷_____ a party at home on my 16ᵗʰ birthday, but my parents said no. It was embarrassing ⁸_____ my friends, but they didn't seem to mind. My parents chose ⁹_____ me for a pizza (boring!), but I was amazed ¹⁰_____ they had organised a surprise party for me at the pizza restaurant with all my friends!

## Infinitives vs. *-ing* forms

**4** ⋆ (Circle) **the correct options.**

1 I really enjoyed (going) / to go to the firework display.

2 It was expensive **getting / to get** in to the festival, but my parents offered **paying / to pay** half.

3 She can't stand **singing / to sing** in a karaoke.

4 **Putting / To put** up the decorations took us three hours!

5 I didn't expect **seeing / to see** you wearing a tuxedo!

6 Would you like **coming / to come** to the party with me?

7 We decided **celebrating / to celebrate** the end of term by **having / to have** a barbecue.

8 I'm looking forward **to being / to be** on holiday next month.

**5** ⋆⋆ **Complete the conversation with infinitives and *-ing* forms. Use the verbs in brackets.**

**Ada:** What's the matter Brad? You look worried.

**Brad:** Yes, I am! I've been chosen ¹ __*to organise*__ (organise) the class end-of-exams celebration, and I'm not very good at ²_____ (have) ideas. What shall I do?

**Ada:** Well, I wouldn't do anything without ³_____ (ask) people what they'd like ⁴_____ (do) first.

**Brad:** Are you offering ⁵_____ (help)? That would be great!

**Ada:** Oh, all right! So now you don't need ⁶_____ (worry), OK?

**Brad:** Actually, it's not that difficult ⁷_____ (guess) what most people in our class would enjoy ⁸_____ (do).

**Ada:** No, ⁹_____ (go) to a theme park is usually at the top of the list!

**Brad:** Yes, and whatever we do, everyone will just be looking forward to ¹⁰_____ (have) a great time after ¹¹_____ (finish) our exams.

**Ada:** Exactly – so relax. It's all going to be fine!

**6** ⋆⋆⋆ **Complete the sentences for you.**

1 I never go out without _____ .

2 One day, I'd like _____ .

3 I never enjoy _____ .

4 One thing I don't like about this age is _____ _____ .

5 This year, I hope _____ .

6 When you're a teenager, it's difficult _____ _____ .

*I never go out without taking my phone with me.*

# Reading

**1** ⭐ **Read the travel website about New Year destinations. Match the cities with the pictures (1–6).**

# Seeing in the New Year

Do you dream of spending New Year's Eve somewhere exciting? Here are some suggestions of iconic places to celebrate New Year. *Take your pick!*

**New York City, USA** – Pictures _4_ and ___ .

Over a million people participate in celebrations all over the city, but the most famous place to *see in* the New Year is Times Square. The tradition began in 1904, but the 'ball drop' started in 1907, when setting off fireworks was *banned*. At exactly 11.59 pm, a large ball, *illuminated* with bright lights, is lowered down the side of the Times Tower building, and 60 seconds later it stops to signal the end of one year and the beginning of the next. The ball drop has become famous all over the world, and nowadays there are fireworks, too! It's crowded but cold, so wear a coat, hat and scarf.

`Click here for more information`

**Rio de Janeiro, Brazil** – Pictures ___ and ___ .

Because it's summer in Brazil, Copacabana Beach in Rio has one of the biggest New Year's Eve parties in the world. Many people wear white clothes to symbolise a new start, and some people bathe in the sea or float candles on the water. Over 2 million people stand on the shore to view the totally stunning fireworks display at midnight. Of course there's also traditional Samba music and dancing to make sure you have a good time!

`Click here for more information`

**Edinburgh, Scotland** – Pictures ___ and ___ .

Hogmanay is the Scottish name for New Year's Eve, a very important celebration in Scotland. Edinburgh's Hogmanay is a three-day event which starts with a colourful Torchlight Procession, music and fireworks. Then there's a Keilidh, a traditional party with Scottish music and dancing, as well as a pop concert and a street party. At midnight on New Year's Eve, join 80,000 people singing the traditional New Year's song, Auld Lang Syne, based on a Scottish poem and folk song. On New Year's Day, there's the Loony Dook, a (quick!) swim in the freezing River Forth *in aid of* charity, or you could just go down to the beach to watch!

`Click here for more information`

**2** ⭐⭐ **Complete the sentences with the words in bold from the text.**
1 Cars are _____ in the shopping streets of the city centre in many cities.
2 At Christmas, the trees are _____ with hundreds of colourful bulbs.
3 We're organising a charity singing contest _____ UNICEF.
4 On New Year's Eve, my parents let us stay up until midnight to _____ the New Year.
5 You can have any of the food here. Just _____ .

**3** ⭐⭐ **Read the website again and answer the questions. Write *NY* for New York, *R* for Rio de Janeiro or *E* for Edinburgh.**
1 Which celebration doesn't involve going in water?          _*NY*_
2 Which celebration lasts the longest?          ___
3 Which celebration has the most people?          ___
4 Which celebration doesn't have music?          ___
5 Which celebration involves doing something to help other people?          ___
6 Which celebration often means wearing clothes of one colour?          ___
7 Which celebration is over a hundred years old?          ___
8 Which celebration has the most impressive fireworks?          ___

**4** ⭐⭐⭐ **What are the New Year traditions where you live? Which destination would you choose for a New Year's Eve celebration and why?**

# Writing

## A description

**1** Read Tania's description. What was the party for and who went?

It was our last year in school and most of us would be going to university or trying to find a job. Our class decided to have a party and luckily the school let us use the school hall. We put up some decorations and our parents made some food, which was all ¹___*so*___ delicious!

Everybody dressed up for the occasion – it was ²_____ funny to see all my classmates in party clothes. First, we watched a video one of our classmates had made with photos of us all from previous years – my friend Chloe said it was ³_____ sad and she started to cry! Then the head teacher came and made a short speech, wishing us all good luck and she told us not to be ⁴_____ noisy!

After that, the DJ played the music we all like and we danced until 9 o'clock. It was ⁵_____ amazing! Some of my friends went to Sam Carter's house after the party but I was ⁶_____ tired, so Chloe and I walked home. It was a great night!

**2** Read the description again. Answer the questions.

1 Where did they have the party?
*They had the party in the school hall.*

2 Who made the food?
_____

3 What did Tania find funny?
_____

4 Why did Chloe start to cry?
_____

5 What did the head teacher tell them to do?
_____

6 Why didn't Tania go to the party at Sam Carter's house?
_____

**Useful language** *so* or *too* + adjective

**3** Complete Tania's description with *so* or *too*.

**4** Circle the correct words.
1 All the presents I was given were **so** / **too** amazing!
2 We wanted to invite Amy but it was **so** / **too** late. She'd already made plans.
3 We thought the fireworks would be **so** / **too** noisy but nobody complained.
4 Greg is **so** / **too** creative – he has lots of ideas for the party.
5 At the beginning it was a bit **so** / **too** quiet but then I put some music on.

> **WRITING TIP**
>
> Make it better! ✓ ✓ ✓
> When *that* is the object of the verb in a relative clause, we don't need it.
> *She was the only person **that** didn't dress up for the occasion.*
> *The music **that** he wanted to play is impossible to dance to.*

**5** Read the sentences. Do you need *that* in the relative clauses?
1 We all went into the hall that was at the back of the hotel. ___*Yes*___
2 We watched a video that my cousin had made. _____
3 On the table there was a huge cake that my mum had baked. _____
4 I danced with some friends that knew my sister. _____
5 My granddad told us a few stories about my dad that we'd never heard. _____
6 The DJ that played at the party was a friend of ours. _____

# Writing

**6** **Complete the sentences with *then* or *after*.**

1 ___After___ lunch, we all went into the garden.

2 I opened my presents and _____ everyone sang 'Happy Birthday'.

3 _____ we'd eaten the turkey, my dad set off some fireworks in the garden.

4 First, we put up some decorations and _____ we prepared the food.

5 My dad made a speech and _____ that, we sat down to eat.

6 _____ the band started playing and everyone got up and danced.

> **WRITING TIP**
>
> **Make it better! ✓ ✓ ✓**
> Give some background information at the beginning of the description saying what the celebration was for.
> *I had just celebrated my 16th birthday and my friends wanted to give me a surprise.*

**7** **Match the sentence beginnings (1–5) with the sentence endings (a–e).**

1 It was my granddad's 80th birthday, ___b___

2 My mum and dad ___

3 My Uncle Paul won a prize ___

4 It was the World Cup Final, ___

5 My mum was born on the same day as her best friend, ___

a so my friends and I got together to watch it.

b so we all went to his house.

c for his last book.

d so they decided to have a party.

e had been married for 20 years.

**8** **Put the information in the order it appears in Tania's description in Exercise 1.**

> the food
> what they did
> how she felt at the end
> ~~background information~~
> where the celebration was
> the arrangements they made

1 *background information*

2 _____

3 _____

4 _____

5 _____

6 _____

## PLAN

**9** **Think of a celebration you remember as a child. Use the categories in Exercise 8 and make notes.**

## WRITE

**10** **Write a description of the celebration. Look at page 71 of the Student's Book to help you.**

_____
_____
_____
_____
_____
_____
_____
_____
_____
_____
_____
_____
_____
_____
_____
_____
_____

## CHECK

**11** **Check your writing. Can you say YES to these questions?**

- Have you used the ideas in Exercise 8?
- Have you used *so* and *too* + adjective correctly?
- Have you used relative clauses with *that*? Do you need *that*?
- Have you used *then* and *after* correctly?
- Have you given some background information?
- Are the spelling and punctuation correct?

**Do you need to write a second draft?**

# Vocabulary
## Celebrations

**1** **Match the sentence beginnings (1–6) with the sentence endings (a–f).**

1 A week before the festival, a contest     _c_
2 The council put up     ___
3 On festival day, little children give a     ___
4 The local shops make     ___
5 People dress up for     ___
6 Everyone at the festival has a     ___

a special cakes for the festival.
b the occasion in traditional costumes.
c is held to find the festival king and queen.
d good time. I love it!
e present they make at school to their parents.
f decorations all over the town centre.

| Total: 5 |

## Descriptive adjectives

**2** **Put the letters in order to make adjectives.**

1 We all went on the ghost train at the fair. It was quite ___scary___ (crays)!
2 It was a really _____ (hatposecrim) show with the music, the lights and the costumes.
3 There are so many tourists at the festival now, it's too _____ (dewcord).
4 We had a birthday picnic in the mountains by a lake. It's a _____ (facepelu) place.
5 We have a _____ (troladitain) medieval festival every May, with dances, games and food.
6 The dancers wore _____ (fullroocu) costumes and threw flowers.

| Total: 5 |

# Language focus
## -ing forms

**3** **Complete the sentences using the -ing form of the verbs in brackets.**

1 I'm looking forward to ___seeing___ (see) my cousins at the celebrations.
2 Next month, my grandparents celebrate _____ (get) married fifty years ago!
3 _____ (study) for exams is boring, but I like _____ (celebrate) when they're finished.
4 Most of my friends enjoy _____ (swim) in the harbour on New Year's Day.
5 I'm quite good at _____ (cook) but I hate _____ (chop) onions.

| Total: 6 |

# Infinitives

**4** **Complete the text using the infinitive form of the verbs in the box.**

> make   remember   earn   provide   ~~give~~
> organise (x2)   set up   dance   think

It's not difficult [1] ___to give___ a good party. You need [2] _____ the guests with plenty of food and drink, but most people just want [3] _____ to good music, and talk to old friends or make new ones. When I was twenty, I offered [4] _____ a friend's 18th birthday party, as he had exams. I thought it was important [5] _____ it was his party, not mine, but in fact he gave me some money and I was expected [6] _____ all the decisions. The party was a big success, and because of that several people asked me [7] _____ their next party. After a few months of this, I decided [8] _____ my own party business. Of course, I'd like [9] _____ lots of money from this, but it's also great [10] _____ that your job is making people happy.

| Total: 9 |

## Infinitives vs. -ing forms

**5** **Circle the correct options.**

I used to love [1]**to celebrate** / **celebrating** my birthday with my family, but now I'm 15, I want [2]**to have** / **having** a party with my friends. My older brother offered [3]**to talk** / **talking** to my parents, and after [4]**to think** / **thinking** about it, they agreed I could have a party at home. I think it's important [5]**to organise** / **organising** things properly, so I asked my mum [6]**to help** / **helping** me get it ready, as it was my first party. We agreed that [7]**to prepare** / **preparing** the food is her responsibility, and the decorations and music are my job. I'm really excited about [8]**to have** / **having** it!

| Total: 7 |

# Language builder

**6** (Circle) the correct options.

**Amber:** What the matter, Kylie? You look a bit worried.

**Kylie:** Mum and Dad want me ¹___ my birthday celebrations myself this year, but I don't know what to do. I have a different idea every week!

**Amber:** Yes, ²___ what to do is hard. When is your birthday?

**Kylie:** Not for ages, April 20th. If it ³___ your party, what would you do?

**Amber:** I'm not sure. I ⁴___ have a party at home. Is that what you're thinking of ⁵___ ?

**Kylie:** No, I'd like to do something a bit different. I ⁶___ for an activity ⁷___ we can have fun and learn something at the same time. There's a new indoor climbing centre near our school. They do a special half-day 'birthday party', where everything ⁸___ for you, including a climbing lesson, lunch and a cake. What do you think?

**Amber:** That sounds good! How many people ⁹___ to invite?

**Kylie:** I've made a list of about 10, including you, of course! I've only got one worry, though. It ¹⁰___ fun unless everyone likes climbing!

**Amber:** Mmm, yes I see what you mean. Maybe you need to find out!

**1 (a)** to organise     **b** organising
   **c** organise       **d** will organise
**2 a** decide         **b** I decide
   **c** deciding      **d** to decide
**3 a** will be        **b** was
   **c** would be     **d** is
**4 a** would        **b** can
   **c** might        **d** will
**5 a** doing         **b** do
   **c** to do        **d** to doing
**6 a** look          **b** 've been looking
   **c** looks        **d** had looked
**7 a** who          **b** what
   **c** where       **d** whose
**8 a** is organised    **b** organise
   **c** will organise   **d** organising
**9 a** you are going   **b** do you
   **c** are you going   **d** will you
**10 a** could be      **b** won't be
    **c** will be       **d** might be

Total: 9

# Vocabulary builder

**7** (Circle) the correct options.

**1** He's ___ confident about the contest! He's sure he's going to win!
   **a** a bit       **b** kind of      **c** extremely
**2** Can you ___ a cake?
   **a** roast      **b** chop       **c** bake
**3** The home-made bread looked a bit strange but it tasted ___ , and I had two slices.
   **a** salty      **b** delicious     **c** disgusting
**4** The festival was really ___ and we had a great time.
   **a** exciting    **b** bored       **c** excited
**5** When are they going to ___ the fireworks?
   **a** put up    **b** set off      **c** give up
**6** The carnival parade is extremely popular so the streets were very ___ .
   **a** peaceful    **b** scary       **c** crowded
**7** The concert finished at 2 am. It was ___ late for a school night, so we didn't go.
   **a** totally    **b** much too    **c** quite
**8** Our students are hard-working and incredibly ___ .
   **a** motivated    **b** shy       **c** easy-going
**9** My mum says we will ___ from your house at 6 pm to go to the party.
   **a** get you up    **b** give you up    **c** pick you up
**10** I was really disappointed ___ the fireworks this year.
   **a** of       **b** by       **c** for

Total: 9

# Speaking

**8** **Put the words in the correct order to make phrases for helping someone to do something.**

**1** my / you / house / to / later / come / Would / ?
   *Would you come to my house later?*

**2** I / costume / help / Can / make / your / you / ?

**3** help / like / if / I'll / you / you

**4** drive / there / you / your / Could / parents / to / ask / us / ?

**5** pair / Shall / baggy / you / lend / a / I / of / trousers / ?

**6** pirate / I / your / borrow / hat / Could / ?

Total: 5

Total: 55

## -ing forms

Remember that:
- we use -ing forms after prepositions. Remember to use the correct preposition.
  ✓ We don't believe *in* spending lots of money.
  ✗ We don't ~~believe spending~~ lots of money.

**1 Complete the sentences with the correct preposition.**

1 We're really looking forward ____*to*____ going to the festival.
2 My brother says I'm really bad _____ organising parties.
3 They spent a lot of money _____ hiring a DJ.
4 I think you'd be really good _____ cliff diving.
5 My brother isn't really interested _____ cliff diving, but his girlfriend loves it.
6 They believe _____ spending time together as a family.
7 She was really happy _____ going to the prom.

**Spell it right!** Regular verbs ending in -y

Remember:
For verbs with two or more syllables ending in a <u>consonant + y</u>:
- In continuous tenses and the -ing form, add -ing
  ✓ study → studying    ✗ study → ~~studing~~
- In the present simple and past simple, replace the -y with -ies or -ied
  ✓ study → studied    ✗ study → ~~studyed~~

For verbs with two or more syllables ending in a <u>vowel + y</u>:
- In continuous tenses and the -ing form, add -ing
  ✓ enjoy → enjoying    ✗ enjoy → ~~enjoing~~
- In the present simple and past simple, add -s or -ed
  ✓ enjoy → enjoyed    ✗ enjoy → ~~enjoied~~

For verbs with <u>one syllable ending in -y</u>:
- In continuous tenses and the -ing form, add -ing
  ✓ pay → paying    ✗ pay → ~~paing~~
- In the present simple, add -s
  ✓ pay → pays    ✗ pay → ~~pais~~
- In the past simple, replace the -y with id
  ✓ pay → paid    ✗ pay → ~~payed~~

**2 Complete the text with the correct form of the verbs in brackets. Check your spelling!**

This summer, when we finish ¹ __*studying*__ (study), my friends are planning to have a party on the beach. When they asked me, I ² _____ (say) we should invite everyone in our class, but they didn't agree. They wanted to invite only their favourite classmates. I ³ _____ (try) to explain that it wouldn't be fair, but they weren't ⁴ _____ (pay) attention to me. So, while they are ⁵ _____ (play) volleyball and ⁶ _____ (enjoy) themselves on the beach, some of our classmates will be at home feeling upset! I've decided not to go to the party!

## Infinitives vs. -ing forms – *like* and *would like*

Remember that:
- we use *like* to talk about something or someone we enjoy or approve of. We use *like* + the -ing form.
  ✓ I *like* **shopping** for new clothes.
  ✗ I *like* ~~shop~~ for new clothes.
- we use *would like* to say politely that we want to do or have something. When *would like* is followed by a verb, we always use the infinitive with *to*.
  ✓ I'd *like* **to go** to Tony's party this weekend.
  ✗ I'd ~~like go~~ to Tony's party this weekend.
  ✗ I'd like ~~going~~ to Tony's party this weekend.

**3 Circle the correct option.**

1 I really like **watch** / **watching** cliff diving. It's so exciting!
2 Would you like **coming** / **to come** to a party at my school?
3 If you come to visit me next summer, what would you like **to do** / **do**?
4 They don't like **help** / **helping** with the party organising, but they love parties!
5 Do you think Julian would like **to go** / **go** to the festival with us?
6 He doesn't really like **visit** / **visiting** museums, but he accepted my invitation!
7 I've always liked **swim** / **swimming**, so I would like to **try** / **trying** diving.

# Weird and wonderful

## Vocabulary

### Story elements

**1** ⭐ **Use the clues to complete the crossword.**

Across row: ³s u s p e n s e

**Across**

**3** a scary feeling before something happens
**6** the _____ is the person who does bad things
**7** the exciting events in a book or film
**8** something no one can explain

**Down**

**1** the place where the events happen
**2** the _____ is the person who saves everyone
**4** the main _____ is the person the story is about
**5** the basic events in the story

**2** ⭐⭐ **Circle the correct words.**

**1** My mum reads detective novels. She likes guessing who the **villains** / heroes are.
**2** Most teenagers like films with a lot of **plot / action** because they're more exciting.
**3** I prefer books where the main **characters / villains** are young people like me.
**4** The **setting / plot** was so complicated that I couldn't follow what was happening.
**5** No one knew when the real painting had been stolen. It was a complete **mystery / suspense**.
**6** The **setting / action** was Australia at the end of the 19th century. It was a violent place!

**3** ⭐⭐ **Match the sentence beginnings (1–6) with the sentence endings (a–f).**

**1** The action was     _b_
**2** The setting was     ___
**3** I couldn't stand     ___
**4** The man who caught the robber     ___
**5** He was the most evil     ___
**6** The plot took     ___

**a** villain I've ever seen.
**b** fast and dramatic!
**c** was a hero.
**d** the suspense, it was so exciting!
**e** a small village in Scotland.
**f** a very unexpected turn at the end.

**4** ⭐⭐ **Complete the text with the correct form of the words in Exercise 1.**

The ¹___*setting*___ for *The Maze Runner* is the Glade, a strange place that a group of teenagers (there are no adults) have to escape from. How they can do that is a(n) ²_____ which they have to solve. The idea was brilliant, but I thought a few of the ³_____ didn't have enough personality, and the ⁴_____ , Thomas, who had lost his memory, seemed to do things a bit too easily sometimes. The ⁵_____ was impossible to predict though, with lots of unexpected turns, and the director really managed to maintain the ⁶_____ right until the end. The ⁷_____ , the Grievers, who are half animal half machine, were very scary too, and the ⁸_____ was fast-moving and exciting. I loved it!

**5** ⭐⭐⭐ **Write answers to the questions.**

**1** Do you prefer books or films with complicated plots or simple ones? Why?
**2** What three elements are most important for you in a film? What about a book?
**3** Do you think heroes or villains are more interesting characters? Why?

*I prefer books with complicated plots because you can go back and check things …*

# Language focus 1

## Third conditional

**1** ⭐ **Complete the rules in the table.**

| | |
|---|---|
| **1** | To form a third conditional sentence, use: *if* + _____ for the situation, and *would(n't)* + _____ + _____ for the result. |
| **2** | We use the third conditional to talk about imaginary situations in the _____ . |
| **3** | We often use the third conditional to talk about things we _____ doing. |

**2** ⭐⭐ **Match the sentence beginnings (1–6) with the sentence endings (a–f).**

1  If the hero hadn't saved them,       ***b***
2  I would have enjoyed the book more  ___
3  If there had been more suspense,  ___
4  If you hadn't lent me the DVD,  ___
5  She wouldn't have read the book  ___
6  Would they have caught the villain  ___

a  the film would have been scarier.
b  they would all have been killed.
c  if she hadn't seen the film first.
d  if he hadn't attacked again?
e  if I'd liked the main characters.
f  I'd never have watched that film.

**3** ⭐⭐ **Write third conditional sentences with the prompts.**

1  Thomas / not end up / in the Glade / if / the Creators / not choose / him
  ***Thomas wouldn't have ended up in the Glade if the Creators hadn't chosen him.***

2  JK Rowling / become / a millionaire / if / Harry Potter / sell / fewer copies?
  _____
  _____

3  If / Edward's family / not save / Bella / vampires / kill / her
  _____
  _____

4  Tris / die / if / Four / not rescue / her
  _____
  _____

5  If / Hazel / not meet / Gus / she / not visit / Amsterdam
  _____
  _____

6  Katniss / not volunteer / for the Hunger Games / if / her sister's name / not be / picked
  _____
  _____

**4** ⭐⭐⭐ **Write third conditional sentences about the story. Use the information given.**

When we bought a new car, we decided to go out for the day.

1  *If we hadn't bought a new car, we wouldn't have gone out for the day.*

Our neighbour said Byrony Lake was lovely, so we went there.

2  _____
  _____

We hired a rowing boat. On the boat, my mother lost her ring in the water.

3  _____
  _____

We all liked Byrony Lake, so we went there again a few weeks later.

4  _____
  _____

We took our fishing rods and caught five fish!

5  _____
  _____

We cooked them for supper. Dad found Mum's ring inside his fish!

6  _____
  _____

## 🔍 Explore prepositions and adverbs of movement

**5** ⭐⭐ **Circle the correct words in the story.**

Andrea stepped ¹**off** / **above** the train in Rio nervously, and looked ²**towards** / **around** her. She was going to university at last, but her cousin wasn't there to meet her as he'd promised. She could just get back onto the train and go ³**through** / **back** home, but she was too excited. She walked slowly along the platform ⁴**towards** / **off** the exit. The big clock hanging ⁵**around** / **above** the platform said 4.55. The train had arrived early! Then she saw her cousin. He was pushing his way ⁶**through** / **off** the passengers, waving and calling her name. Her adventure was beginning!

# Listening and vocabulary

## Listening

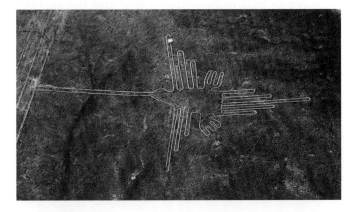

**1** ★ 🔊 **07** **Listen to a radio programme called Unexplained Mystery. Put the topics in the order the presenter talks about them.**

a how the lines were made ___
b why the lines were made ___
c where the lines are ___
d the shapes the lines make ___

**2** ★★ 🔊 **07** **Listen again and choose the correct options.**

1 The Nazca lines are found in Peru …
   ⓐ in the desert.
   b close to Lima.
   c north of the desert.

2 The lines are mysterious because … on the ground.
   a you can't see the lines
   b you can't see any shapes
   c you can only see some shapes

3 The shapes the lines made were discovered …
   a in the 1920s.
   b by an archaeologist.
   c when they were seen from the air.

4 The big shapes are …
   a lots of different things.
   b all animals and birds.
   c difficult to recognise.

5 The figures were made …
   a with red sand.
   b by local people.
   c in the first century AD.

6 The lines have existed for over 1,500 years because …
   a they were a heritage site.
   b lots of people looked after them.
   c there is no wind or rain.

7 Which of these is <u>not</u> a theory about the Nazca lines?
   a They were underground lakes.
   b They were to guide UFOs.
   c They were for studying the stars.

## Linking phrases

**3** ★ **Complete the definitions with the words in the box.**

> true   alternative   cause   obvious
> wanted   why   ~~opposing~~   said

1 *then again* introduces a(n) __*opposing*__ opinion
2 *rather than* explains a(n) _____ action
3 *in fact* emphasises that something is _____
4 *according to* explains who _____ something
5 *as a result of* explains the _____ of an action
6 *of course* says that what you are saying is _____
7 *in order to* explains _____ someone did something
8 *so that* explains what someone _____ to do

**4** ★★ **Circle the correct options in the text.**

[1]**According to** / **Rather than** their website at www.ripleys.com, Robert Ripley started his weird and wonderful 'Believe it or not' newspaper column in the USA in 1918. [2]**In order to** / **As a result of** its popularity, he soon needed many more true stories and facts. [3]**So that** / **Rather than** find them himself, Ripley hired a man called Norbert Pearlroth to look for information. [4]**In fact** / **Of course**, poor Norbert spent the next 52 years in the New York Public Library working 10 hours a day, 6 days a week [5]**in order to** / **according to** find unusual facts for Ripley. Later came radio and TV programmes, comics, books and even museums around the world [6]**so that** / **in fact** people could enjoy all the strange stories Ripley and Pearlroth found. [7]**Of course** / **Then again**, Ripley's team insisted that all the information was true, but many things are hard to believe. [8]**As a result of** / **Then again**, they do say that life is stranger than fiction, so who knows?

# Language focus 2

## must have, can't have, might/may/could have

**1** ★ (Circle) the correct words in the table.

| | |
|---|---|
| **1** | To talk about possible explanations in the past, we use a modal verb + infinitive / *have* + past participle. |
| **2** | We use *must* / *can't* / *might, may* and *could* to say an explanation is the only possibility. |
| **3** | We use *must* / *can't* / *might, may* and *could* to say an explanation is possible. |
| **4** | We use *must* / *can't* / *might, may* and *could* to say an explanation is impossible. |

**2** ★ (Circle) the correct words.
1 You **must** / **can't** have seen the Yeti! It doesn't exist!
2 The 'lion' in the woods **might** / **must** have been a domestic cat. It's the only explanation!
3 It's possible that the strange object in the sky **could** / **can't** have been a UFO.
4 I thought she **might** / **must** have been French but I wasn't sure.
5 The man said they **might** / **can't** have seen him because he was at home watching TV.
6 You **must** / **may** have discovered a prehistoric cave painting. We need to do tests to find out.

**3** ★★ Write sentences with the prompts in brackets to answer the questions.
1 How did the thief get into the house? (He / might / have / a key)
*He might have had a key.*
2 Why didn't the alarm go off? (The thief / must / switch off)
_____
3 Why didn't he steal the other painting? (It / may / be / too heavy)
_____
4 When did the robbery happen? (It / could / happen / Friday or Saturday)
_____
5 Why did the police find his fingerprints? (He / can't / wear / gloves)
_____
6 Why was his phone outside the house? (He / must / drop it)
_____
7 So how did the police find him? (It / can't / be / very difficult)
_____
8 Why haven't they found the painting? (He / might / hide it / or / could / sell it)
_____

**4** ★★ Complete the text with *must have, can't have* or *might/may/could have* and the correct form of the verbs in the box.

> have ~~build~~ transport use be bury

Stonehenge, the remains of two huge stone circles, is a prehistoric monument in the south of England. Scientists analysing the stones say that the Neolithic people ¹ _**must have built**_ it between 2,500 BC and 1,500 BC. They brought enormous stones from Wales, a journey of about 385 kilometres, but they ² _____ the stones all the way on land, because they were too heavy. Experts now think they took them most of the way by sea and river on boats. Everyone agrees that Stonehenge ³ _____ an important monument, because it's so big, but no one knows exactly what it was for. There are various theories. It ⁴ _____ religious significance, or people ⁵ _____ their dead there, as many bones have been found. Because of how the sun shines through the stones, others say that the Neolithic people ⁶ _____ Stonehenge as a solar calendar to follow the changing seasons. One thing is sure, though, it will always be a mystery!

**5** ★★★ Think about the people who lived in your country several thousand years ago. Write at least five sentences about what life was like then. Use the ideas in the box or your own ideas and *must have, can't have* and *might/may/could have.*

> food entertainment diseases
> houses work education visitors

*People can't have had a very healthy life because there were no medicines or hospitals.*

# Reading

**1** ★ **Read the profile of a young writer. Tick (✓) the kind of books she writes.**

children's stories ☐    short stories ☐
crime ☐    mysteries ☐
fantasy ☐    biographies ☐

## DO IT YOURSELF

Anna Caltabiano was born in Hong Kong to a Japanese mother and an Italian-American father, and spoke Mandarin Chinese at school. Then she moved to Palo Alto, California. An only child, Anna loved reading, and started writing short stories as soon as she could write. She wasn't very sociable, and she had a weird habit of talking **out loud** to herself, so every year her parents signed her up for summer camp, which she hated, so she could make friends.

Then, when she was thirteen, Anna **made a deal** with her parents: instead of summer camp, she would stay at home and write a novel. They could have said no but, surprisingly, they agreed. Of course, if her parents *had* said no, she probably wouldn't have published her first novel at 14. Every morning that summer, Anna sat at the table with her tablet and a cup of tea. She used a short story she'd written, and worked in an unusual way. First she drew pictures of her ideas, then she wrote them down. She wrote dialogue by texting it to herself on her mobile phone. It wasn't the 'normal' way to write a novel, but it helped her to develop the plot and the action.

The setting for *All That Is Red* is a **futuristic** world, like something from a dream, where 'red' and 'white' are fighting a war. Anna uses red to represent human emotions, and white to represent 'nothingness', the complete absence of things. In the story, the main character doesn't know which side she belongs to and is stuck between these two worlds. It's a fantasy story, but the theme relates to how teenagers feel growing up.

Originally, Anna thought just writing the book would be enough, but then she realised she wanted other people to read it. After hundreds of **rejection letters** from **publishers**, most people might have given up, but Anna decided to publish it herself, with great success! She has now finished a second novel *The Seventh Miss Hatfield*, another fantasy involving immortality and time travel, and is writing another. Not bad for 17!

**2** ★★ **Complete the sentences with the correct form of the words in bold from the text.**

1 Mara, can you read your story _____ to the class? Listen everyone.
2 The _____ of this book is Cambridge University Press.
3 Let's _____ . If I help you with the Maths homework, you can help me with English.
4 Science-fiction novels are always set in a(n) _____ society, often on other planets.
5 After getting three _____ from universities, she was finally accepted by another.

**3** ★★ **Read the profile again. Complete the table with information about Anna.**

| Name | Anna Caltabiano |
|---|---|
| Age | |
| Family | |
| Place of birth | |
| Home | |
| Education | |
| Hobbies | |
| Books | |

**4** ★★ **Answer the questions.**

1 Why did Anna's parents send her to summer camp every summer?
*Because they wanted her to make friends.*
2 What was the deal that Anna made with her parents?
_____
3 What is unusual about how she writes?
_____
4 What is the theme of her first book?
_____
5 What happened after she received the rejection letters?
_____

**5** ★★★ **Would you be interested in reading Anna's books? Why/Why not? Have you ever read any books by a teenage author? Which? What was it like? If you wrote a book, what kind would you write?**

# Writing

## Telling a story

**1** **Read Christine's story. What happened to her?**

It was a really windy day but my dad said because it was Sunday, we should go for a walk. He wanted to go to the beach, but we went to the park because my mum said it might be less windy there. My sister and I were walking a little bit ahead of our parents when, ¹**luckily / suddenly**, we heard a really loud noise. A huge branch from a tree had crashed to the ground behind us.

I ²**immediately / eventually** turned around. I couldn't see my parents and, ³**obviously / fortunately**, I thought the branch had fallen on them. I panicked a bit at first but then I realised that, ⁴**luckily / suddenly**, they had stopped to look at the ducks and the branch had missed them.

Just then, we saw a man climbing out from under the leaves. ⁵**Eventually / Amazingly**, he wasn't hurt because, ⁶**obviously / fortunately** for him, only the lighter parts of the branch had fallen on him.

⁷**Eventually / Amazingly**, the firefighters came and cut the branch into smaller pieces and moved it out of the way. It could have been a lot worse. That man was so lucky, he could have been killed by that branch.

**2** **Read the story again. Put the events in the correct order.**

a Christine turned around to look for her parents. ___
b Christine and her sister walked in front of her parents. ___
c A man came out from under the branch. ___
d Christine's parents stopped to look at the ducks. ___
e The firefighters came to move the branch away. ___
f Christine and her family went for a walk. _1_
g A branch fell off a tree. ___

**Useful language** Adverbs _____

**3** **Read Christine's story again. Circle the correct words.**

**4** **Complete the sentences with adverbs from Exercise 3. There is more than one possible answer.**

1 _Suddenly,_ everyone stopped what they were doing.
2 _____ no one was hurt.
3 _____ an ambulance came and took him to hospital.
4 _____ we couldn't go on with our trip, so we went home.
5 _____ he got up and walked away as if nothing had happened!

# Writing

**5** **Match the sentence beginnings (1–5) with the sentence endings (a–e).**

1 It all happened so quickly ___*d*___
2 He was walking so slowly ___
3 She was cycling so fast ___
4 She shouted so loudly ___
5 He behaved so badly ___

a that everyone turned around to look at her.
b that she couldn't stop.
c that even his mother was shocked.
d that I couldn't react.
e that I thought he was hurt.

**6** **Circle the correct words.**

1 They ran **quick** / **quickly** and caught the bus.
2 We were really **lucky** / **luckily** that the weather was so good.
3 They were cycling around the park when **sudden** / **suddenly** it started raining.
4 It was such a **loud** / **loudly** noise that everyone jumped.
5 She spoke so **quiet** / **quietly** that nobody could hear her.
6 It couldn't have been a more **amazing** / **amazingly** day.

> **WRITING TIP**
>
> Make it better! ✓ ✓ ✓
> Talk about possible consequences at the end of your story using *could have*.
> It **could have** *been a real disaster, but everything was all right in the end.*

**7** **Complete the sentences with *could have* and the correct form of the verbs in the box.**

| lose   break   hurt   ~~be~~   miss |

1 It ___*could have been*___ much worse.
2 He _____ himself badly but he was OK.
3 She _____ everything she had that day.
4 We _____ the bus but fortunately it arrived late.
5 I _____ my leg but luckily it was only a small cut.

**8** **Read Christine's story in Exercise 1 again and tick (✓) the information she includes.**

background information ☑
descriptive adjectives ☐
adverbs ☐
a variety of past tenses ☐
what happened in the end ☐
what people said ☐

## PLAN

**9** **You're going to write a story that ends with the sentence: *It could have been much worse.* Use the items in Exercise 8 and make notes.**

## WRITE

**10** **Write your story. Look at page 83 of the Student's Book to help you.**

_____
_____
_____
_____
_____
_____
_____
_____
_____
_____
_____
_____
_____
_____
_____

## CHECK

**11** **Check your writing. Can you say YES to these questions?**

- Have you included all the information in Exercise 8?
- Has your story got a beginning, a middle and an end?
- Have you used adverbs with *so* in your story?
- Have you used adjectives and adverbs correctly?
- Have you finished your story with a possible consequence?
- Are the spelling and punctuation correct?

**Do you need to write a second draft?**

# Vocabulary
## Story elements

**1** Circle the correct options.

1 Nowadays, a lot of the action / plot in films is done using special effects.

2 The villain / plot in the Harry Potter books is called Voldemort.

3 The setting / suspense went on for so long I was terrified.

4 The main characters / mysteries are a group of people who survived a terrible virus.

5 I would like to see more female villains / heroes saving the world in comics.

6 The mystery / setting is a tropical island where there are many strange animals.

7 The plot / heroes of this book is similar to Romeo and Juliet, the Shakespeare play.

8 In the film, the mystery / action is solved by two teenage fans of CSI.

| Total: 7 |

## Linking phrases

**2** Complete the text with the phrases in the box.

> in fact   rather than   as a result of   in order to
> then again   of course   ~~so that~~   according to

A cat in Sydney called Churchill had a lucky escape recently. His owner had roasted a chicken and left it on the table ¹___so that___ it could cool a little. Churchill stole it. ²_____ , his owner shouted at him, and ³_____ that, Churchill ran next door – into Taronga Zoo! ⁴_____ escape from his owner, Churchill ran straight into the bears' cage, and hid behind a bear that was finishing its dinner. But the bear was friendly. ⁵_____ , they even shared the chicken together. ⁶_____ the zoo keeper, it was lucky that Churchill chose the bears ⁷_____ the tigers. The tigers hadn't had their dinner! But ⁸_____ , maybe tigers like roast chicken too!

| Total: 7 |

# Language focus
## Third conditional

**3** Write third conditional sentences using the prompts.

1 If / Churchill / be / outside / he / not see / the chicken
   *If Churchill had been outside, he wouldn't have*
   *seen the chicken.*

2 If / he / not steal / the chicken / his owner / not shout / at him
   _____

3 If / he / run / in the other direction / he / not go into / the zoo
   _____

4 The tigers / eat / him / if / he / run / into their cage
   _____

5 If / I / see / the cat and the bear together / I / be / amazed
   _____

6 I / not believe / the story / if / there / not be / a photo
   _____

| Total: 5 |

## *must have, can't have, might/may/could have*

**4** Complete the conversation with *must have, can't have* and *might/may/could have* and the correct form of the verbs in brackets.

**A:** I didn't understand the plot of that film. Did you?

**B:** Yes, I'd seen it before.

**A:** Ah … so who was the man in the mask?

**B:** Good question. That part was a bit confusing. I suppose it ¹ *might have been* (be) the murderer, or it ²_____ (be) the private detective who was looking for the girl who had disappeared. I wasn't sure.

**A:** Well, it ³_____ (be) the detective, because he was at the police station.

**B:** Oh, yes, you're right. So it ⁴_____ (be) the murderer. But what was he doing there?

**A:** I can't imagine. The writers ⁵_____ (make) a mistake, I suppose. Apparently, they often change things when they are still filming, so it's easy to get things wrong!

**B:** Yes, and they ⁶_____ (realise) when they were editing the film or they would have cut that bit out. Or was it part of the story?

**A:** I thought you said you understood the plot!

| Total: 5 |

## Language builder

**5** (Circle) the correct options.

Since 1903, when it was first suggested, scientists ¹___ to develop a flying car that you can drive or fly, but for many years it ²___ impossible. Then, in 2013, a European company ³___ that they had finally produced a test model of a flying car. It was developed in the Czech Republic by AeroMobil, a company ⁴___ chief designer first worked on a flying car at home with his father when he was a teenager. Perhaps if he ⁵___ interested in the idea then, he wouldn't have spent so much time and money on the project. Even a few years ago, not many people ⁶___ flying cars except in fantasy films, but now several companies are developing them, and predict that they ⁷___ the way we travel completely. However, if there were cars flying round in the air, ⁸___ dangerous? And where would all the cars land? In any case, AeroMobil hopes ⁹___ the new model in the next two or three years, so we will probably be able to buy the flying car soon after that. Not many people ¹⁰___ them at first, though. According to AeroMobil, the cars ¹¹___ for about $280,000.

| | | | |
|---|---|---|---|
| **1** | **ⓐ** have been trying | **b** | are trying |
| | **c** tried | **d** | try |
| **2** | **a** is seeming | **b** | is being |
| | **c** is | **d** | had seemed |
| **3** | **a** are announcing | **b** | were announcing |
| | **c** announced | **d** | have announced |
| **4** | **a** that | **b** | whose |
| | **c** who | **d** | which |
| **5** | **a** hadn't become | **b** | became |
| | **c** didn't become | **d** | had become |
| **6** | **a** would imagine | **b** | could have imagined |
| | **c** must imagine | **d** | can't have imagined |
| **7** | **a** change | **b** | won't change |
| | **c** might change | **d** | can change |
| **8** | **a** wouldn't it be | **b** | it would be |
| | **c** will it be | **d** | it won't be |
| **9** | **a** testing | **b** | to test |
| | **c** test | **d** | will test |
| **10** | **a** bought | **b** | will be buying |
| | **c** are buying | **d** | buying |
| **11** | **a** are going to sell | **b** | will sell |
| | **c** will be sold | **d** | are sold |

Total: 10

## Vocabulary builder

**6** (Circle) the correct options.

**1** Did you ___ a good time at the film festival?
  **a** spend     **b** hold     **ⓒ** have

**2** It was a very ___ book. It really made life on the island seem real.
  **a** suspense     **b** atmospheric     **c** traditional

**3** Jimmie is having a horror party for his birthday, and we have to ___ for the occasion.
  **a** dress up     **b** put up     **c** sign up

**4** I thought the action scenes in the film were really ___ . It was great!
  **a** disappointed   **b** impressive     **c** boring

**5** The main character was ___ to save the people in her village. It was inspiring.
  **a** business     **b** determined     **c** strict

**6** The ___ for the story was a safari park in Botswana, in Africa.
  **a** setting     **b** plot     **c** action

**7** ___ the film, many people read the book it was based on.
  **a** So that     **b** In order to     **c** As a result of

**8** They ___ to drive to the mountains early in the morning.
  **a** set off     **b** looked round   **c** picked up

Total: 7

# Speaking

**7** **Put the sentences in the correct order to make a conversation.**

___ **A:** Well, I decided to walk back through the park, and I found her bike by the lake!

_1_ **A:** I nearly got into big trouble yesterday.

___ **A:** Well, I borrowed my sister's bicycle to go to the shop.

___ **A:** No! So I didn't ask her. Anyway, I was only in the shop for a minute, but when I came out, the bike was gone.

___ **A:** I know! Extremely lucky! I rode home quickly before anything else happened.

___ **A:** No, I didn't tell her. If she'd found out, she'd have been really angry!

___ **B:** Did your sister find out?

___ **B:** Does she let you borrow it?

___ **B:** Wow! That was lucky!

___ **B:** Really – why was that?

___ **B:** Oh no! So then what happened?

Total: 10

Total: 51

## Third conditional

> Remember that:
> - we use **if + past perfect** to describe the imaginary past situation. We do not use *would* in the *if* clause.
>   ✓ *If my friend **hadn't called**, …*
>   ✗ *If my friend ~~wouldn't have~~ called, …*
>   ✗ *If my ~~friend called~~, …*
> - we use **would (+ not) + have + past participle** to express an imaginary past result we feel sure of.
>   ✓ *…, I **would have stayed** at home.*
>   ✗ *…, I ~~had stayed~~ at home.*
>   ✗ *…, I ~~stayed~~ at home.*

**1 Are the sentences correct? Rewrite the incorrect sentences.**

1 If you had been at the concert, you had enjoyed it too.
*If you had been at the concert, you would have enjoyed it too.*

2 If she arrived later, it would have been impossible to save her life.

3 The book would have been better if the hero wouldn't have died.

4 If we had worked together, we would have finished the project sooner.

5 I missed my friends if I had gone on holiday with my parents.

6 If they would have known the film was so exciting, they would have gone to see it.

7 We wouldn't have found the house if you didn't sent us a map.

## must have, can't have, might/may/could have

> Remember that:
> - we use *might, may, could, can* and *must* **+ have + past participle** to explain why something has happened or suggest what has happened.
>   ✓ *He **must have jumped** out of the plane.*
>   ✗ *He ~~must jumped~~ out of the plane.*
>   ✗ *He must have ~~jump~~ out of the plane.*

**2 Find and correct seven more mistakes in the conversation.**

Lisa: Have you seen my dog, Bobby?
Ben: No. When did you last see him?
Lisa: He was playing in the garden. He must ~~had~~ₐ *have* escaped.
Ben: Could someone have leave the gate open?
Lisa: I don't think so. It's always locked. He can't jumped over the gate. It's too high!
Ben: Do you think he might have go under it?
Lisa: No … Someone must opened the gate.
Ben: He might has hidden somewhere in the garden. Have you looked everywhere?
Lisa: Yes, of course. I suppose my mum might have came home at lunchtime. Maybe she took him for a walk? I'll call her.
Ben: Don't worry! He can't have go far!

## Linking phrases – *in order to* and *so that*

> Remember that:
> - we use *in order to* and *so that* with a similar meaning to explain why we do something. But we use them in different ways.
> - we use *so that* **+ clause**. Remember to use *so*.
>   ✓ *Finn built the causeway **so that he could trick** his enemy.*
>   ✗ *Finn built the causeway ~~in order~~ he could trick his enemy.*
> - we use *in order to* **+ infinitive**. Remember to use *to*.
>   ✓ *Finn built the causeway **in order to trick** his enemy.*
>   ✗ *Finn built the causeway ~~so that~~ to trick his enemy.*

**3 Circle the correct option.**

1 He built a time machine **so that / (in order to) / in order** travel back in time.

2 They must have taken the gun **in order to / so that / that** they could kill the monster.

3 I gave him my phone number **in order that / in order / so that** he could contact me directly.

4 Tell me what time your train arrives **so that / in order to / that** I can come to meet you.

5 He got up early **in order / in order to / so that** to prepare for his lessons.

6 **In order to / In order / So that** cross the river, they had to build a boat.

7 You have to call them first **in order / in order to / so that** to get an appointment.

# 8 Right or wrong?

## Vocabulary

### Crimes

**1** ★ **Add vowels to make words for crimes.**

1 pckpcktng _____pickpocketing_____
2 kdnppng _____
3 rbbry _____
4 vndlsm _____
5 llgl dwnldng _____
6 rsn _____
7 shplftng _____
8 mggng _____

**2** ★ **Match the words in Exercise 1 with the definitions.**

1 taking things from a building _____robbery_____
2 stealing from a supermarket _____
3 damaging things in a public place _____
4 watching films you didn't pay for on your computer _____
5 attacking someone to steal from them in the street _____
6 stealing from a pocket or bag in a public place _____
7 starting a fire deliberately to destroy something _____
8 taking a person away by force _____

**3** ★★ **Complete the sentences with the words in Exercise 1.**

1 After the _kidnapping_ , the man's family paid $100,000 to get him back.
2 There's a lot of _____ in the town centre, so be careful – watch your purse.
3 The firefighter said it was definitely _____ . They found petrol on the floor.
4 There was a(n) _____ in our street yesterday. The attacker stole my neighbour's phone.
5 Clothes shops often attach little plastic security tags to clothes to stop _____ .
6 Film companies say that _____ damages the film industry.
7 He spent several months planning the bank _____ .
8 There's a lot of _____ in the town centre. Yesterday, the bus station was damaged.

**4** ★★ **Complete the texts about crime.**

I live in a big city. Here ¹ _shoplifting_ is common, both in big shopping centres and small shops. ² _____ is also frequent, especially stealing wallets from tourists, and at night in some areas ³ _____ is a problem, so I never walk home alone. Of course, the most common crime these days is probably ⁴ _____ of songs and films, but, for some reason, many people don't consider that a crime at all!

I live in the country, so there isn't much crime. There was a(n) ⁵ _____ at a farm in the summer, but they didn't steal very much. When I was little, we had a forest fire which everyone said was ⁶ _____ , but they never caught anyone. Oh, yes, last year there was an attack of ⁷ _____ when someone threw paint at the bus stop. Boring, but I suppose we're lucky really!

**5** ★★★ **Write about where you live. Is it more like A or B in Exercise 4? Why? Are any of the crimes in Exercise 1 rare in your country? What crimes have you heard about recently? Write at least five sentences.**

*Last month, there was a robbery at my school. The thieves stole some computers.*

# Language focus 1

## Reported statements

**1** ⭐ **Complete the rules in the table.**

| | |
|---|---|
| **1** | When we report a conversation, we can use the verbs _____ or _____ . |
| **2** | The verb _____ must be followed by a direct object, but the verb _____ has no direct object. |

**2** ⭐ (Circle) **the correct words in the text.**

He ¹**told /** **said** that his name was Julio, and ²**said / told** us that he was a tourist. Then he ³**said / told** that he didn't speak much English. He was hurt, so I ⁴**said / told** him that he needed to wait while I phoned for an ambulance. They ⁵**said / told** that it would take ten minutes. I tried to ⁶**say / tell** Julio that the ambulance wouldn't be long, but he was unconscious. Finally, the ambulance came and took him to hospital. The paramedics ⁷**said / told** us that we didn't need to worry, and that he would be OK. Let's hope so.

**3** ⭐⭐ **Complete the reported statements.**

1 'I think it's wrong to download songs without paying,' said Errol.
   Errol said that he ___*thought it was*___ wrong to download songs without paying.

2 'I ran after the pickpocket but I didn't catch him,' the boy told us.
   The boy told us that he _____ after the pickpocket but that he _____ him.

3 'Although the cameras can't stop crime, they will help catch more criminals,' he said.
   He said that although the cameras _____ crime, they _____ catch more criminals.

4 'I've reported the robbery to the police,' she said.
   She said that she _____ the robbery to the police.

5 'The robbers broke into the school through a window,' the head teacher said.
   The head teacher said that the robbers _____ into the school through a window.

6 'Crimes on property aren't as serious as crimes against people,' Karl said.
   Karl said that crimes on property _____ as serious as crimes against people.

**4** ⭐⭐ **Read this report by a store detective. Write what the girl said.**

1 The teenager said that she was innocent.
   '*I'm innocent.*'

2 She told me that she hadn't stolen any sweets.
   _____

3 She said that she had her little brother with her.
   _____

4 She told me that he had put the sweets in her bag.
   _____

5 She said that she would put them back.
   _____

6 She told me that she could pay for them.
   _____

**5** ⭐⭐⭐ **Read what a witness said to a police officer. Then complete the report.**

> My name is Darren Smith. I live at number 27, Owen Road. I saw a car stop outside number 29 at about 8 o'clock last night. I've seen it before. It's a black Mercedes. I don't know the number. A man got out and went into the house. I can't remember what the man looked like. I'll ask my wife when she comes home.

The witness said that ¹___*his name was*___ Darren Smith, and that ²_____ at number 27, Owen Road. He told me that ³_____ a car stop outside number 29 at about 8 o'clock on the night of the kidnapping. He said that ⁴_____ before, that ⁵_____ a black Mercedes, but that ⁶_____ the number. He said that ⁷_____ and gone into the house. He told me that ⁸_____ what the man looked like. He told me that ⁹_____ his wife when ¹⁰_____ home.

**6** ⭐⭐⭐ **Think of a short conversation you had today and report it.**

*I told my mum I'd be home late after school because I had drama club. Dad said he could pick me up if I ...*

# Listening and vocabulary

## Reporting verbs

**1** ★ **Match the reporting verbs in the box with the people's statements.**

> decide explain ~~suggest~~ admit
> insist promise agree complain

**1** 'Why don't you watch this programme
about crime?'                    _suggest_

**2** 'I'll pay you back the money next
month.'                    _____

**3** 'Yes, I think you're right.'         _____

**4** 'It happened when I was on my way
home from school.'            _____

**5** 'I'm definitely going to be more
careful now.'                _____

**6** 'Yes, it was me. I started the fire.'  _____

**7** 'You must go to the police. You have
to report it.'               _____

**8** 'The police don't do anything!
There should be more of them on
the streets.'                _____

**2** ★★ **Complete the text with the correct form of the verbs in Exercise 1.**

Last year, thieves broke
into my house and stole
my laptop, TV and some
jewellery. I went to
the police station and
¹ _explained_ that I'd
been broken into. They
² _____ that they
would investigate, but
when a police officer
came round, he was only
there for five minutes,
and ³ _____ that there was nothing he
could do. I ⁴ _____ that that wasn't a proper
investigation, and I ⁵ _____ that he sent
someone to look for fingerprints. Eventually, the
officer ⁶ _____ that he would. They found
lots of fingerprints and the thief was actually on
their database. When they went to his house, he
⁷ _____ that he had stolen my things and
amazingly, I got everything back. When I thanked
the police, I ⁸ _____ that they would catch
more criminals if they investigated crimes like this
more seriously. Not all robbers are clever enough to
wear gloves!

## Listening

**3** ★ 🔊 **08** **Listen to a conversation about restorative justice. What is it?**

**a** bigger punishments for crimes, decided by
the victim

**b** victims and criminals meeting to explain their
lives to each other

**c** criminals admitting their crimes and doing
community service

**4** ★★ 🔊 **08** **Listen again and complete the sentences.**

**1** According to the article, a new restorative justice
scheme will begin _____ _next year_ _____ .

**2** The scheme brings together _____
and _____ to talk.

**3** The officially organised meeting is called a
_____ .

**4** Victims can explain _____ made
them feel and the damage the crime had on their
_____ .

**5** The offender can explain why _____
and _____ to the victim.

**6** Justin thinks this is _____ and would
be _____ .

**7** Sometimes there is an agreement
to _____ money or do
_____ work in the community.

**8** In the survey in New Zealand, 77% of victims said it
_____ .

**9** The scheme is _____ , and a meeting
only happens if everyone _____ .

**10** Offenders who go through this process are 25%
_____ to break the law again.

# Language focus 2

## Reported questions

**1** ★ (Circle) the correct words in the table.

| | |
|---|---|
| **1** | When we report a question, we usually use the verb *ask / tell*. |
| **2** | In reported *Yes/No* questions, we put the word *that / if* after the reporting verb. |
| **3** | In a reported question:<br>• we **change / don't change** the tense of the direct question.<br>• the word order **is / isn't** the same as the direct question.<br>• the **subject / verb** comes before the **subject / verb**.<br>• we **use / don't use** an auxiliary verb.<br>• we **put / don't put** a question mark. |

**2** ★ **Read the direct questions from a police interview. Complete the reported questions.**

**1** 'Where did the mugging take place?'
The detective asked me *where the mugging had taken place* .

**2** 'Have you noticed anyone following you?'
She asked me _____ .

**3** 'Can you describe the man?'
She asked me _____ .

**4** 'What kind of phone is it?'
She asked me _____ .

**5** 'Do you have a tracker app on your phone?'
She asked me _____ .

**6** 'What did the man say?'
She asked me _____ .

**7** 'Did you see anyone else?'
She asked me _____ .

**8** 'Where can I contact you?'
She asked me _____ .

## Indirect questions

**3** ★ **Complete the rules in the table.**

| | |
|---|---|
| **1** | Indirect questions, start with a phrase like *'Can/Could you _____ me … ?'* or *'I _____ wondering …'*. |
| **2** | In *Yes/No* questions, we use the word _____ in the indirect question. |
| **3** | In an indirect question:<br>• the word order is like a _____ not a question.<br>• we put the subject before the _____ .<br>• we _____ an auxiliary verb. |

**4** ★★ **Look at the direct questions in brackets. Then complete the indirect questions.**

**1** Can you tell me *where the police station is?*
(Where is the police station?)

**2** I was wondering _____
(Could I ask you a few questions?)

**3** Could you tell me _____
(What did the man look like?)

**4** Do you know _____
(How much was there in the wallet?)

**5** Can you tell me _____
(Had you seen the man before?)

**6** I was wondering _____
(Why didn't you call the police then?)

**7** Could you tell me _____
(Where did you get off the bus?)

**8** Do you know _____
(What time was it?)

**5** ★★★ **Imagine you are a journalist. Think of three indirect questions you might ask a police officer about a crime. Then report three questions you have been asked today.**

*Can you tell me how many suspects there are?*

*My boss asked me if I had finished the article on the kidnapping.*

## Explore verb expressions

**6** ★★ (Circle) **the correct options in the text.**

The US legal system ¹**went ahead / (dates back to)** 1787, when the American Constitution was signed. However, it didn't actually ²**come into existence / see the point** until four years later, when all the states agreed to use it. In the USA, although each state can make its own laws, they must ³**take care / run out of** not to go against the Constitution. Activists can challenge new state laws by going to the Supreme Court in Washington. If the Supreme Court judges ⁴**see the point / take care** of their arguments, then the state has to abolish the new law. With criminal cases, not all states work in the same way. In some states, a criminal prosecution will only ⁵**date back to / go ahead** if a jury accepts it and, in fact, 90% of criminal cases are never heard by a judge or jury, because a sentence is agreed out of court. However, although there are fewer crimes now than 25 years ago, it seems the courts will never ⁶**run out of / come into existence** cases.

# Reading

**1** ★ **Read the true story of a young detective. Tick (✓) the evidence she found.**

a footprint ☐  the robbers' names ☐  a broken window ☐

the stolen things ☐  some fingerprints ☐  a key ☐

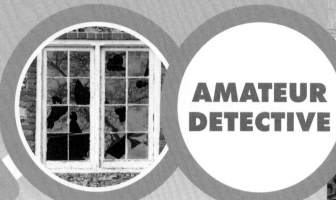

# AMATEUR DETECTIVE

Not many people get the chance to be an amateur *sleuth*, but that's exactly what happened to American teenager Jessica Maple. What's more, she actually solved the crime before the police.

A few weeks after Jessica's great-grandmother died, there was a robbery at her house, and some furniture was stolen. When the police investigated the robbery, they looked around the house. Because they didn't see any broken windows or doors, they quickly decided that there had been no *forced entry*, and that the thieves must have had a key to the house. Jessica didn't agree. She knew that there were only two keys, and her parents had one each. So she decided to investigate the crime herself.

First, she went to her great-grandmother's house to look for clues. At the side of the house was a garage, and it *turned out* that the garage windows had been broken. When Jessica looked inside, she saw that everything in the garage was on the floor, so the thieves must have been in there. When she looked more carefully, she found fingerprints in the dirt around the window.

Then Jessica had an idea. She knew there was a second-hand furniture store near her great-grandmother's house, so she went to look for the stolen furniture. Amazingly, it was all there on sale. So she told the shop manager who it belonged to, and explained that thieves had stolen it. The manager told Jessica that he knew who the thieves were, because they had often brought him furniture. When Jessica asked what their names were, he told her, and even found their addresses for her. Jessica took all the evidence she'd collected to the police, who were amazed!

That wasn't the end of the story though. Jessica and her mother visited one of the robbers and asked him why he'd done it. Although he *denied* the offence at first, he finally admitted that it was him. Jessica had solved the crime! She told reporters that she had learned her *investigative skills* at a camp that summer, but she hadn't expected to use them quite so soon!

**2** ★★ **Match the words in bold in the text with the definitions.**

1 a detective _____

2 say that you didn't do something _____

3 getting into a building by damaging or breaking something _____

4 have a particular result _____

5 abilities that help someone to find out about a crime or mystery _____

**3** ★★ **Read the story again and put the events in the correct order.**

a The robber said he was guilty. ___  g Jessica spoke to one of the robbers. ___

b The police came. ___  h Jessica found important evidence. ___

c Jessica spoke to the manager. ___  i Jessica went to the police. ___

d There was a robbery. ___  j Jessica didn't agree with the police. ___

e Jessica went to summer camp. *1*  k Jessica went to a shop. ___

f The police said the robber used a key. ___  l Jessica found out the robbers' names. ___

**4** ★★★ **Do you think Jessica was right to investigate the robbery herself? And to visit the thief? Why do you think the police were surprised? Were the thieves good at what they did? Write at least five sentences.**

# Writing

## A news article

**1** Read the text. Where do you think it appeared?

# ROCKVILLE SHOPLIFTERS?

Recently, there have been some reports in the local newspaper about shoplifting in the area around our school. The reports suggest that our friends and classmates may be responsible. Is it true? Are students from Rockville School really stealing from the local shops? We went to find out.

First, we carried out a survey among students at the school to find out if anyone was involved in activities like stealing. In fact, well ¹___*over*___ 90% of the students said they had never stolen anything in their lives and about ²_____ quarters of them said that they had an excellent relationship with the shop owners near the school.

So we asked the shop owners what they thought. Two ³_____ of them, a clear majority, insisted that they thought the shoplifting wasn't really done by students from our school. Only ⁴_____ five of them complained that Rockville students make a lot of noise in the shops, but ⁵_____ under 90% of them (88%) admitted that the relationship was actually excellent and the students' behaviour was generally very good.

So now everyone wants to know why the local newspaper is suggesting that Rockville students are stealing from shops around the school. The investigation continues.

**2** Read the article again. Are these sentences true or false? Correct the false sentences.

**1** The local newspaper says Rockville students are involved in vandalism. ✗
*The local newspaper says Rockville students are involved in shoplifting.*

**2** Most Rockville students say they never steal anything.

_____

**3** Both students and shop owners say the relationship between them is very good.

_____

**4** All the shop owners complain about the noise the students make.

_____

**5** The article gives information that is very different from the information in the local newspaper.

_____

**Useful language** Describing amounts

**3** Complete the article with the words in the box.

> about   just   thirds   ~~over~~   three

**4** Write sentences based on the information. Use the words in brackets.

**1** students we talked to who have never stolen anything in their lives – 95% (an estimated)
*An estimated 95% of students we talked to have never stolen anything in their lives.*

**2** students at our school who recycle – 68% (just under)

_____

**3** people in the school who think it's wrong to download illegally – between 48 and 53 (approximately)

_____

**4** students in our survey who have downloaded music from the Internet – 52% (just over)

_____

**5** students who were at the demonstration – 38 or 39 (about)

_____

**6** students who have been robbed – 6 (well under)

_____

> **WRITING TIP**
>
> Make it better! ✓ ✓ ✓
> We use the present perfect to describe changes.
> *The problem **has become** worse and worse in recent years.*

# Writing

## 5 Write present perfect sentences with the prompts.

1 Sales of DVDs / fall / over the last few years
*Sales of DVDs have fallen over the last few years.*

2 Illegal downloading / rise / in the last decade
_____

3 The size of our class / go up / in the last five years
_____

4 Many shops / open / in this area recently
_____

5 A lot of small businesses / close this year
_____

## 6 Circle the correct options.

1 Everybody **know** / **knows** that it is illegal to download music without paying.

2 **All the people** / **Everyone** uses the Internet for downloading apps.

3 **All the students** / **All students** we talked to insisted it wasn't true.

4 **Every** / **All** student knows the school rules.

5 Nobody **want** / **wants** to pay more money for music or apps.

> **WRITING TIP**
>
> Make it better! ✓ ✓ ✓
> Start your article with one or two questions and then try to answer them in the article.
> *Why has illegal downloading increased so dramatically recently?*

## 7 Put the words in order to make questions.

1 broken / you / the / Have / law / ever / ?
*Have you ever broken the law?*

2 this / explain / Can / situation / anyone / ?
_____

3 still / online / pay / content / Do / for / young / people / ?
_____

4 cinema / have / recently / Why / audiences / decreased / ?
_____

5 real / for / What / young / the / nowadays / is / people / situation / ?
_____

## 8 Read the article in Exercise 1 again and order the sections (A–D).

A Second argument/point – with examples and figures _____

B Introduction – with questions _____

C Conclusion – with consequence or result _____

D First argument/point – with examples and figures _____

## PLAN

## 9 You're going to write an article for your school newspaper. Choose one of the ideas below or your own idea. Then use the paragraphs in Exercise 8 and make notes.

- There have been reports of vandalism in the area.
- Some students have been mugged near the school.
- A lot of people think all students download music illegally from the Internet.
- A lot of students complain that there's nothing to do in the neighbourhood.

## WRITE

## 10 Write your article. Use the structure in Exercise 8 and page 93 of the Student's Book to help you.

_____
_____
_____
_____
_____
_____
_____
_____
_____
_____
_____
_____
_____
_____
_____
_____

## CHECK

## 11 Check your writing. Can you say YES to these questions?

- Have you used the structure in Exercise 8?
- Have you used different phrases to describe amounts to support your points?
- Have you used the present perfect to describe changes?
- Have you used quantifiers and indefinite pronouns correctly?
- Have you started your article with a question or some questions?
- Have you written a conclusion explaining the consequence or result?
- Are the spelling and punctuation correct?

**Do you need to write a second draft?**

## Vocabulary
### Crimes

**1** Circle the correct options.
1 Everyone was shocked by the robbery / kidnapping of the baby from his garden.
2 There is a lot of **pickpocketing / arson** in tourist areas these days.
3 There was some **vandalism / shoplifting** in the city centre after midnight last night.
4 The forest fire last week was **mugging / arson**, according to the fire service.
5 There was a(n) **robbery / illegal downloading** last night at a bank in King Street.

Total: 4

### Reporting verbs

**2** Complete the sentences with the correct form of the verbs in the box. There are three extra words.

> agree ~~promise~~ suggest decide admit
> explain insist complain

1 I _promise_ that I will contact you immediately if the man comes back to the shop.
2 Yes, I _____ that the crime must have been committed by a family member.
3 When she spoke to the police, the witness _____ that she had seen everything.
4 Can I _____ that you don't leave your passport or money in your hotel room?
5 The thief _____ that he couldn't keep the stolen items, so he sold them.

Total: 4

## Language focus
### Reported statements

**3** Complete the reported statements.
1 'Our town doesn't have a lot of crime.'
They said that _their town didn't have a lot of crime_ .
2 'I watch a lot of detective drama on TV.'
He said that _____ .
3 'I can remember the number of his car.'
She said that _____ .
4 'We haven't downloaded many songs illegally.'
They said that _____ .
5 'We will catch the person who attacked you.'
The police told him that _____ .

Total: 4

## Reported questions

**4** Complete the text by reporting the questions.
1 'How long have you known Mr Forbes?'
2 'When did you last see him?'
3 'Is he in trouble?'
4 'Have you noticed anything unusual recently?'
5 'What can you remember about last Tuesday?'
6 'Why is last Tuesday important?'
7 'Will you look at some photos?'
8 'Do you recognise any of these men?'

The detectives asked me [1] _how long I had known_ Mr Forbes, and [2] _____ .
So I asked them [3] _____ and they said he had disappeared. Then they asked me [4] _____ anything unusual and [5] _____ about last Tuesday.
I asked them [6] _____ and they told me that he had probably disappeared on Tuesday afternoon. Then they asked me [7] _____ some photos and [8] _____ any of the men, but I didn't. I don't think I was much help to the investigation.

Total: 7

## Indirect questions

**5** Complete the conversation with indirect questions.

**Ed:** Hello, I was wondering [1] _if I could have some information_ . (Could I have some information?) Could you tell me [2] _____ (Do I need a degree to become a CSI?)

**Careers Advisor:** Yes … in Forensic Science.

**Ed:** Do you know [3] _____ (Do I have to be a police officer?)

**CA:** No, not necessarily.

**Ed:** And I was wondering [4] _____ (How long does all that take?)

**CA:** Well, probably four or five years at least.

**Ed:** Can you tell me [5] _____ (What else do I need?)

**CA:** Yes, you need determination. There are a lot of people interested in each job, so it isn't easy. And can I ask you [6] _____ (Why are you interested in this career?)

**Ed:** Yes, it's because I like the television series!

Total: 5

# Language builder

**6** (Circle) **the correct options.**

A man ¹___ lives in a small town in Ohio was walking home from the supermarket with his shopping when he ²___ a fox. Don King had seen foxes around before, but they always ran away. Not this one, though. It ³___ very hungry. After ⁴___ at the fox didn't work, Mr King said that he ⁵___ it some food. 'In the end, I threw it some biscuits, and it ran away. If I hadn't given it some food, it ⁶___ stopped. I'd have been badly injured, as it was quite large and aggressive.' I asked a wildlife expert ⁷___ an unusual event. She told me that foxes ⁸___ be afraid of humans, but now that many foxes live in towns, these attacks were happening more often. She suggested that if people find ⁹___ in this kind of situation, a water pistol is best to frighten an aggressive fox. Perhaps after his experience, Mr King ¹⁰___ for one next time he goes shopping.

| | | | |
|---|---|---|---|
| 1 | **a** whose | **b** which | |
| | **c** where | **ⓓ** who | |
| 2 | **a** was attacked by | **b** attacked | |
| | **c** was attacked | **d** attacked by | |
| 3 | **a** had been | **b** wasn't | |
| | **c** must have been | **d** can't be | |
| 4 | **a** to shout | **b** he shouted | |
| | **c** shouted | **d** shouting | |
| 5 | **a** had given | **b** was giving | |
| | **c** has given | **d** has been giving | |
| 6 | **a** must have | **b** would have | |
| | **c** can't have | **d** wouldn't have | |
| 7 | **a** why was this | **b** if this was | |
| | **c** if was this | **d** where this was | |
| 8 | **a** used to | **b** were | |
| | **c** would | **d** used | |
| 9 | **a** themselves | **b** yourself | |
| | **c** yourselves | **d** himself | |
| 10 | **a** is looking | **b** would look | |
| | **c** will be looking | **d** looks | |

Total: 9

# Vocabulary builder

**7** (Circle) **the correct options.**

1 After stopping a gang of robbers, Mrs Timson was a ___ .
   **a** villain      **ⓑ** hero      **c** character

2 After meeting a victim of a mugging, the mugger decided to ___ crime.
   **a** give up      **b** set off      **c** switch off

3 The man wouldn't ___ that he was shoplifting, and said it was a mistake.
   **a** admit      **b** complain      **c** explain

4 Crime here isn't getting worse. ___ , there's a lot less now.
   **a** Of course      **b** So that      **c** In fact

5 It's a ___ how the criminals were able to escape so quickly.
   **a** suspense      **b** mystery      **c** stunning

6 Many people who know illegal ___ is against the law, don't think it's really a crime.
   **a** mugging      **b** kidnapping      **c** downloading

7 After the mugging, he was ___ upset to sleep that night.
   **a** a bit      **b** much too      **c** really

8 Why are you so ___ in true crime programmes? I think they're boring.
   **a** interested      **b** fascinated      **c** keen

Total: 7

# Speaking

**8 Complete the conversation with the phrases in the box.**

> rumours are completely false   ~~is it true~~   absolutely
> like to comment on   is that right
> they're totally untrue   must be joking

**Reporter:** Josie, ¹____*is it true*____ that you're giving up pop music to go into acting?

**Josie:** No. I'm going to do both!

**Reporter:** And you're moving to Hollywood.
²_____ ?

**Josie:** You ³_____ ! I've just bought a villa in the south of France.

**Reporter:** Oh, right. Would you
⁴_____ the rumours that your parents have stolen a lot of your money?

**Josie:** Yes, I would.
⁵_____ . I get on very well with my parents.

**Reporter:** What about the rumours that you've left your record company?

**Josie:** Those ⁶_____ , too.

**Reporter:** So life is the same as always?

**Josie:** Yes, ⁷_____ !

Total: 6

Total: 46

## Reported statements – *say* and *tell*

Remember that:

- we use *say* + (*that*) clause to report statements. We do not include a direct object.
  ✓ *He **said he would never** do it again.*
  ✗ *He said ~~me~~ he would never do it again.*
- we use *tell* + direct object + (*that*) clause to report statements.
  ✓ *The robber **told reporters** he was innocent.*
  ✗ *The bank robber ~~told he was innocent~~.*
- we use *told* and not *said* to report that someone communicated something, such as a story, a lie, the truth or a secret.
  ✓ *My sister **told** me a lie.*
  ✗ *My sister ~~said~~ me a lie.*

**1** **Find and correct five more mistakes with *say* and *tell* in the email.**

Hi Marco,

I've got a problem. Last weekend, I went to a party.
I ~~said~~ *told* my mum and dad I was doing homework with
Maria. I know I shouldn't have said a lie, but I knew
they would tell I couldn't go to the party. The exams
are soon! Anyway, the party was in the house next
door to my dad's friend's house. He saw me and he
said my mum that I was there. When my mum told
what she had heard, I said it wasn't true. I don't
think they believe me. I feel really bad! If I say them
that I lied, they'll be very angry. What should I do?

James

## Reported questions

Remember that:

- we use the same word order as in affirmative statements when we report questions and we do not add an auxiliary verb.
  ✓ *I asked him **how he caught** the robber.*
  ✗ *I asked him how ~~did he catch~~ the robber.*
- we use *if* when we report questions without a question word.
  ✓ *I asked him **if** he was scared.*
  ✗ *I asked him ~~was he~~ scared.*
- we don't use the preposition *to* after *ask*.
  ✓ *They asked me why I was there.*
  ✗ *They asked ~~to~~ me why I was there.*
- we don't use a question mark at the end of reported questions.

**2** **Are the reported questions correct? Correct the incorrect questions.**

1 The police officer asked me where did I live.
   *The police officer asked me where I lived.*

2 My teacher asked me if have I any plans for the summer holidays.
   _____

3 I asked my parents could I go to the party.
   _____

4 They asked me if I would like to visit them next summer.
   _____

5 My teacher asked me why am I always late for lessons.
   _____

6 My mum and dad asked to me where was I last night.
   _____

## crime

Remember that:

- we use *crime* (without *the* or *a*) to talk about illegal activities in general.
  ✓ *CCTV cameras often help prevent **crime**.*
  ✗ *CCTV cameras often help prevent ~~the~~ crime.*
- we use *the crime* to talk about a particular crime we have mentioned before, and *a crime* or *crimes* to talk about particular examples of criminal activity.
  ✓ *Graffiti is **a crime** in a lot of countries.*
  ✗ *Graffiti ~~is crime~~ in a lot of countries.*
- we use the verb *commit* with *crime*. We do not use *do* or *make*.
  ✓ *I am guilty of **committing** the crime.*
  ✗ *I am guilty of ~~doing~~ the crime.*
- we use *criminal(s)* to talk about people who commit a crime. We always use the plural (with *-s*) or *the/a* when we talk about someone like this.
  ✓ *The police said he was **a criminal**.*
  ✗ *The police said he ~~was criminal~~.*

**3** **Circle the correct option.**

1 In the past, the level of **crime** / **criminal** in this city was very high.

2 Illegal downloading is **the / a** very modern crime.

3 What would you do if you saw **a / the** criminal in the street?

4 There should be more serious punishments for people who **commit / do** crimes.

5 Kidnapping is a very serious **criminal / crime** in most countries.

6 It is the job of the police to fight **the crime / crime**.

# Speaking extra

## Buying clothes

**1** ★ ▶ **1.3** **Put the words in order to make sentences.**

**1** pop / crazy / Mum / music / was / about
_____

**2** weren't / into / My / that / music / parents
_____

**3** disco / I / they / guess / liked
_____

**4** the Beatles / were / grandparents / into / My
_____

**5** into / My / Michael Jackson / both / parents / were / really
_____

**6** that / were / punk music / with it / They / went / and / into / everything
_____

**2** ★ 🔊 **09** **Listen to the conversation. What is the relationship between the boy and the girl?**

**3** ★★ 🔊 **09** **Complete the conversation with the words in the box. Then listen again and check.**

| looks   changing   size   suits   fit   about |

**Girl:** So, you've got a pair of jeans. Let's find a cool T-shirt for you.

**Boy:** How ¹_____ this one? It's got a big green L on the front!

**Girl:** Yeah, L for 'loser'.

**Boy:** Hey! Come on, you're supposed to be helping me!

**Girl:** Here, try this one.

**Boy:** OK, where are the ²_____ rooms?

**Girl:** Over there. And try this one as well.

**Boy:** So what do you think?

**Girl:** Well, it doesn't ³_____ very well. It's too small for you.

**Boy:** But it's M – medium. It's my ⁴_____ .

**Girl:** Have you put on weight?

**Boy:** Very funny.

**Girl:** Sorry, but it ⁵_____ a bit tight.

**Boy:** I'll try the other one on.

**Girl:** OK, that's better. You look great in that one.

**Boy:** Do you think so? Do you think this colour ⁶_____ me?

**Girl:** Red? Of course … it goes with your red hair!

**Boy:** This is the last time I go shopping with my sister!

## Pronunciation focus

**4** ★ 🔊 **10** **Listen to the sentences. Which words are stressed in each one? Listen and repeat.**

**1** These shoes don't fit me.

**2** I don't think it suits you.

**3** You don't look good in that dress.

**4** This coat is not my size.

**5** I'm not so sure.

**5** ★ 🔊 **11** **Listen to the conversation. What is the problem with the second dress that Amy tries on?**

**6** ★★★ 🔊 **11** **Listen again and complete the conversation.**

**Amy:** Right, Sue, ¹_____ this dress for Sophie's party? I like the stripes.

**Sue:** Yeah, it's a nice dress. But stripy clothes don't ²_____ .

**Amy:** Yeah, you're right and it's a bit short, isn't it?

**Sue:** Hey, look at this one. It's denim but it's a lovely colour.

**Amy:** OK, I think I'll try it on. ³_____ ?

**Sue:** They're over there. I'll be there in a minute.

**Sue:** So, let's see you.

**Amy:** OK, here's the denim dress. What do you think?

**Sue:** Wow! ⁴_____ !

**Amy:** Do you think? I think it's too small.

**Sue:** No, it's definitely ⁵_____ . Not too big here not too small there!

**Amy:** Hold on, I've got another one.

**Sue:** Err … no, that doesn't ⁶_____ . It's really baggy.

**Amy:** What do you mean? It's perfect!

**Sue:** Yes, you're right. It's perfect. But Amy … it's the same dress I'm going to wear to Sophie's party. Sorry.

**7** ★★ 🔊 **11** **Listen again and check your answers. Then listen and repeat the conversation.**

# Speaking extra

## Showing concern

**1** ★ ▶ **2.3** **Complete the sentences with the words in the box.**

> come easier little difficult through helps

1 That seems to help a _____ .
2 I've helped my best friend Kate _____ a lot of things.
3 I can't say I've helped anyone through a _____ situation.
4 I'm a good listener, so my friends always _____ to me with their problems.
5 I've talked to him a lot on the phone and that _____ .
6 I hope that makes it a little _____ .

**2** ★ 🔊 **12** **Listen to the conversation. What's Jo's problem?**

**3** ★★ 🔊 **12** **Complete the conversation with the words in the box. Then listen again and check.**

> worry up mean poor better fine down

**Tim:** What's ¹_____ , Jo?
**Jo:** I told my dad I wanted to give up piano lessons and now he's angry with me.
**Tim:** Oh, you ²_____ thing! Why is he angry?
**Jo:** Well, you know my dad … he's so passionate about music.
**Tim:** Well, I'm sure he'll calm ³_____ soon. Why do you want to give up?
**Jo:** I don't know … it's just that we've got all these exams and I'm trying to study every day and I have piano lessons twice a week. And Chinese classes and hockey at the weekend.
**Tim:** I know what you ⁴_____ . It's really hard to do everything!
**Jo:** And I have to practise this really difficult piece on the piano. I just don't think I'm very talented when it comes to music.
**Tim:** Of course you are. You don't need to ⁵_____ . You're so hard-working. I'm sure you'll learn it.
**Jo:** But I have to play the whole thing tomorrow.
**Tim:** I'm sure it'll be ⁶_____ . Just keep practising. So, how can I make you feel ⁷_____ ?
**Jo:** Can you listen to me play it and tell me … honestly … what you think?
**Tim:** Of course, go on then.

## Pronunciation focus

**4** ★ 🔊 **13** **Listen to the sentences. Do they go up or down? Listen and repeat.**

1 I'm sure it'll be fine.
2 You don't need to worry.
3 I know what you mean.
4 I'm sure she'll calm down soon.
5 Oh! You poor thing.

**5** ★ 🔊 **14** **Listen to the conversation. What happened to Dylan's brother's guitar?**

**6** ★★★ 🔊 **14** **Listen again and complete the conversation.**

**Dylan:** Lewis, you have to help me!
**Lewis:** OK, Dylan, ¹_____ ?
**Dylan:** Remember the other night at my house when I borrowed my brother's guitar?
**Lewis:** Yes, isn't it funny that I have the same guitar as your brother?
**Dylan:** Well, now there's a hole in the back of the guitar. He's really angry!
**Lewis:** Well, I'm sure ²_____ . I've got a hole in my guitar but it doesn't matter really. … That's funny, I can't find it now.
**Dylan:** But now he won't lend me his guitar.
**Lewis:** ³_____ . Do you want to borrow mine?
**Dylan:** Great thanks. But what about my brother?
**Lewis:** Oh, I'm sure he'll ⁴_____ .
**Dylan:** Yes, but he really loves that guitar.
**Lewis:** ⁵_____ make you feel better?
**Dylan:** I don't know … I hate it when I can't talk to my brother.
**Lewis:** I know ⁶_____ . It's awful.
**Dylan:** But how did I make a hole in the guitar?
**Lewis:** You ⁷_____ . He'll soon realise that … Hold on. This isn't my guitar. Look, the strings are different!
**Dylan:** That's my brother's guitar!
**Lewis:** And he has my guitar … the one with the hole!

**7** ★★ 🔊 **14** **Listen again and check your answers. Then listen and repeat the conversation.**

# Speaking extra

## Making decisions

**1** ⭐ ▶ **3.3** **Join the parts of the sentences.**

**1** My favourite band's going to be in town next month
**2** I'm saving up for an electric guitar
**3** I've seen a second-hand one that I really like
**4** I also want to travel some before I start
**5** I get money from doing chores around the house

**a** but it's really expensive.
**b** so I'm saving some of that to help pay for it.
**c** and I don't want to miss that.
**d** so I'm saving for that, too.
**e** so I can play a wider range of songs.

**2** ⭐ 🔊 **15** **Listen to the conversation. What are they trying to decide?**

**3** ⭐⭐ 🔊 **15** **Complete the conversation with the words in the box. Then listen again and check.**

> suggest   way   need   shall   thinking   idea   rather

**Girl:** So, what are we going to buy Mum for her birthday?
**Boy:** Do we have to decide now? I'm in the middle of level 37 of this game!
**Girl:** Level 37? Wow! Anyway, yes, we ¹_____ to decide quickly because her birthday is next Saturday.
**Boy:** OK, well, I was ²_____ of a nice silk scarf or a bag, something like that.
**Girl:** But she's got lots of bags and I think Dad was going to buy her a really expensive one. I think I'd ³_____ buy her something really different – what about a ride in a fast car, like a Ferrari or a Lamborghini? You know she loves cars.
**Boy:** But isn't that really expensive?
**Girl:** It's not that expensive, and I think Gran and Granddad would help us.
**Boy:** Well, if they're going to help us, why don't we give her something really nice?
**Girl:** What kind of thing do you ⁴_____ ?
**Boy:** What about a weekend away in a nice hotel?
**Girl:** Yes, that's a good ⁵_____ , too.
**Boy:** Sometimes I have good ideas, you know!
**Girl:** So how ⁶_____ we decide?
**Boy:** Hmm … good question. Hold on, I think the best ⁷_____ is to ask Mum – she's always good at choosing presents for people.
**Girl:** Yeah, but the present is for her!!!
**Boy:** Oh, yeah!!

## Pronunciation focus

**4** ⭐ 🔊 **16** **Listen to the sentences. Which words are linked? Listen and repeat.**

**1** I was thinking‿of‿buying‿her‿a scarf.
**2** That's a good idea.
**3** Personally, I'd rather go on a holiday.
**4** I think the best way is to ask someone.
**5** What kind of thing do you suggest?

**5** ⭐ 🔊 **17** **Listen to the conversation. What are Oliver and Emily going to talk about in the class presentation?**

**6** ⭐⭐⭐ 🔊 **17** **Listen again and complete the conversation.**

**Oliver:** So, we have to make a presentation to the class and we haven't even thought about what we're going to talk about.
**Emily:** I have thought about it. ¹_____ doing a presentation about interesting celebrations around the world.
**Oliver:** I think Conor and Natalie are going to do that. Personally, ²_____ talk about some different career possibilities in the future. We talked about it one day in social science class.
**Emily:** Oh yeah! ³_____ , too. But do you think it'll be easy to find information?
**Oliver:** Yes, actually, I've already done a bit of research and there's loads of stuff on the Internet.
**Emily:** OK, great. So ⁴_____ who does what. Someone has to write the presentation.
**Oliver:** And we should probably include some pictures.
**Emily:** OK, what kind of pictures ⁵_____ ?
**Oliver:** Hmm … I don't know. We can decide that when the time comes. ⁶_____ who does what, then?
**Emily:** ⁷_____ is for me to let you start and when it's ready I'll make the presentation.
**Oliver:** Ha ha. So I do all the work?
**Emily:** Of course.

**7** ⭐⭐ 🔊 **17** **Listen again and check your answers. Then listen and repeat the conversation.**

# Speaking extra

## Giving instructions

**1** ⭐ ▶ `4.3` **Complete the sentences with the words in the box.**

> skip   get up   vegetarian   choose   stand   dishes

1 I'd cook on a Saturday so I wouldn't have to _____ so early.
2 If I could _____ the meal, I'd pick lunch.
3 We did cooking at school last year, so I can think of a lot of _____ .
4 I can't _____ cooking, so I'd ask my brother to write a menu.
5 I'd _____ breakfast since I never eat it anyway.
6 I'm a _____ , so that would be a problem with my family.

**2** ⭐ 🔊 `18` **Listen to the conversation. What are the girls making?**

**3** ⭐⭐ 🔊 `18` **Complete the conversation with the words in the box. Then listen again and check.**

> stir   thing   Finally   Next   Then   first

**Cerys:** So, are you going to help me or not?
**Sarah:** Yes, of course. What do we need?
**Cerys:** OK, the first ¹_____ to do is get the ingredients. We'll need eggs, flour and sugar …
**Sarah:** … and butter and yoghurt from the fridge. Right. What's next?
**Cerys:** So, ²_____ of all, put the sugar and butter into a bowl and mix them together.
**Sarah:** OK, that's done. What now?
**Cerys:** Now break the eggs and mix those in.
**Sarah:** Yuk, it looks a bit slimy now.
**Cerys:** Well, you haven't finished yet. ³_____ , you add the yoghurt. You need to ⁴_____ it a lot.
**Sarah:** If I had a machine, this would be easier.
**Cerys:** ⁵_____ all you do now is start mixing in the flour.
**Sarah:** Mmm … that's delicious.
**Cerys:** ⁶_____ , when you've finished mixing it, put it in here and spread it out.
**Sarah:** Mmm … OK, hold on, just a little bit more.
**Cerys:** Come on. If you don't put it in the oven to bake now, you'll have nothing left!

## Pronunciation focus

**4** ⭐ 🔊 `19` **Listen to the instructions. Do they go up or down? Which instruction goes down? Why? Listen and repeat.**

1 First of all, mix the ingredients together.
2 Then, put it in the fridge for about 10 minutes.
3 Next, you spread the mix out in here.
4 Finally, put it in the oven for 20 minutes.

**5** ⭐ 🔊 `20` **Listen to the conversation. What are the boys making?**

**6** ⭐⭐⭐ 🔊 `20` **Listen again and complete the conversation.**

**Jamie:** So, do you remember how we made them the last time?
**Paolo:** Yes, of course I remember. It was really easy.
**Jamie:** Good, because you're going to make them this time. So what's first?
**Paolo:** Erm … the ¹_____ is to chop some onions and to fry them a little bit.
**Jamie:** Yes, that's right. Then what?
**Paolo:** ²_____ is to mix the other ingredients together.
**Jamie:** OK, so what are the other ingredients?
**Paolo:** Erm … minced meat, of course. And …
**Jamie:** … bread. Well, breadcrumbs. And one other thing.
**Paolo:** Eggs. So, ³_____ the minced meat, the bread and the eggs together.
**Jamie:** That's right. You need to ⁴_____ . Use your hands.
**Paolo:** ⁵_____ the fried onions.
**Jamie:** Yes. Don't forget to add salt and pepper.
**Paolo:** ⁶_____ , when the mix is ready, I make some balls of meat and hit them with my hand to make them flat.

**7** ⭐⭐ 🔊 `20` **Listen again and check your answers. Then listen and repeat the conversation.**

# Speaking extra

## Buying a gadget

**1** ★ ▶ 5.3 **Join the parts of the sentences.**
1　I actually like it better than my phone
2　I share a room with my brother and
3　It's made for long backpacking trips
4　You can squeeze it really hard and
5　Basically, to turn it off,

a　so it's light and compact.
b　you have to throw it against the wall.
c　since he always goes to bed early I need my light to read.
d　then it just pops back into shape.
e　because it's got a nicer camera.

**2** ★ 🔊 21 **Listen to the conversation. What's the problem with the shop assistant?**

**3** ★★ 🔊 21 **Complete the conversation with the words in the box. Then listen again and check.**

| like　use　much　tell　show　Has　long |
| --- |

**Susie:**　Excuse me, can you ¹_____ me about this tablet?
**Shop assistant:**　Yes, of course.
**Susie:**　How ²_____ memory has it got?
**Shop assistant:**　This one is just 16GB … no 8, sorry … but you can add extra memory because it has a USB port just here… no here on the other side … I think.
**Susie:**　³_____ it got a good camera?
**Shop assistant:**　Yes, it has actually. This one has a 10-megapixel camera. Or is it 8?
**Susie:**　And how ⁴_____ does the battery last?
**Shop assistant:**　About 10 hours of constant use.
**Susie:**　What's the sound ⁵_____ ?
**Shop assistant:**　Well, the good thing about this tablet is that the speakers are at the front. … just here … err, somewhere …
**Susie:**　OK. Could you ⁶_____ me how it works?
**Shop assistant:**　Yes, of course. Just a moment …
**Susie:**　Is it easy to ⁷_____ ?
**Shop assistant:**　Oh yes, just press this button to start. Oh, no, sorry. It's this button here. … No that's the volume. … Err, James, can you help us … sorry about this …

## Pronunciation focus

**4** ★ 🔊 22 **Listen to the questions. Do they go up or down at the end? Listen and repeat.**
1　Could you show me this tablet?
2　How much memory has it got?
3　What's the camera like?
4　Can you tell me about this smartphone?
5　Is it difficult to use?
6　Has it got speakers?

**5** ★ 🔊 23 **Listen to the conversation. Why doesn't Isabelle buy the laptop?**

**6** ★★★ 🔊 23 **Listen again and complete the conversation.**

**Isabelle:**　Excuse me, do you work here?
**Shop assistant:**　Yes, I do. How can I help you?
**Isabelle:**　Well, I'm looking for a good laptop.
**Shop assistant:**　OK, well, we have lots. What kind were you looking for?
**Isabelle:**　Well, I don't really know … I don't know much about computers. What about this one here, ¹_____ this one?
**Shop assistant:**　Yes, this is the new XG 950, it's very fast.
**Isabelle:**　²_____ has it got? I'm only really going to use it for work and to connect to the Internet.
**Shop assistant:**　It's got 1TB. That should be more than enough, I expect.
**Isabelle:**　I'll need to use it when I'm travelling, so ³_____ last?
**Shop assistant:**　It depends on exactly what you're doing, but about 10 hours.
**Isabelle:**　And ⁴_____ the operating system _____ ? Is it easy to use?
**Shop assistant:**　Yes, it's very easy to use, don't worry.
**Isabelle:**　⁵_____ USB ports? I'll need to connect my camera and MP3 player.
**Shop assistant:**　Yes, there are two here and one here on the other side.
**Isabelle:**　And … ⁶_____ ?
**Shop assistant:**　Well, this one is $899.
**Isabelle:**　Oh, could you ⁷_____ ? Maybe a bit cheaper?
**Shop assistant:**　Yes, of course. Now, how much were you thinking of spending?

**7** ★★ 🔊 23 **Listen again and check your answers. Then listen and repeat the conversation.**

# Speaking extra

## Offers and requests

**1** ★ ▶ `6.3` **Complete the sentences with the words in the box.**

> outfit   broke   showed   parents   went   funny

1 Only two other people _____ up.
2 The sound system _____ right at the beginning of the evening.
3 But this time it all _____ wrong.
4 It was horrible and _____ at the same time.
5 I showed up in a lobster _____ .
6 But then her _____ showed up.

**2** ★ 🔊 `24` **Listen to the conversation. Where are Josh and Leo going to buy the present?**

**3** ★★ 🔊 `24` **Complete the conversation with the words in the box. Then listen again and check.**

> shall   borrow   'll   help   Would   ask

**Josh:** Oh, I almost forgot, it's my dad's birthday tomorrow. I haven't got him a present.
**Leo:** Don't worry, you've got lots of time. What are you going to give him?
**Josh:** I've no idea. I was going to buy him a shirt.
**Leo:** Can I ¹_____ you to choose one? I love shopping for clothes!
**Josh:** Great. Let's look on the Internet first. Could I ²_____ your tablet?
**Leo:** Here you are.
**Josh:** ³_____ you come to the shopping centre with me later?
**Leo:** OK, ⁴_____ I ask my mum to drive us there?
**Josh:** That would be brilliant. Could you ⁵_____ her to pick us up later as well?
**Leo:** Sure. Come on, I ⁶_____ help you find a nice shirt online first if you like.
**Josh:** OK. Do you know any good websites? …

## Pronunciation focus

**4** ★ 🔊 `25` **Listen to the sentences. Which words are linked? Listen and repeat.**

1 I'll help‿you if‿you like.
2 Shall I lend you my bike?
3 Could I borrow your laptop?
4 Could you ask your sister to come?
5 Can I help you with the decorations?
6 Would you come to the shopping centre with me?

**5** ★ 🔊 `26` **Listen to the conversation. What are Ana and Milly going to do later?**

**6** ★★★ 🔊 `26` **Listen again and complete the conversation.**

**Ana:** Hi Milly. ¹_____ your Portuguese dictionary?
**Milly:** Yeah, sure. What are you doing?
**Ana:** I'm writing to my pen pal, but I don't know what to say.
**Milly:** I'll help you ²_____ .
**Ana:** No, it's OK. I think I'll leave it until tomorrow. I have to study history for a test.
**Milly:** Well, ³_____ to study for the test?
**Ana:** Great. You're really good at history.
**Milly:** Well, I like it. ⁴_____ you some questions about the chapter?
**Ana:** That's a good idea. But let me study it first. ⁵_____ to my house later?
**Milly:** Sure. ⁶_____ your mum to make some of her delicious pancakes?
**Ana:** I'm afraid not. She's away on a business trip.
**Milly:** Oh no … well, if your mum's not around, I'm not going to your house.
**Ana:** What? So you're not going to help me with my history?
**Milly:** Of course I am, I'm only joking!

**7** ★★ 🔊 `26` **Listen again and check your answers. Then listen and repeat the conversation.**

# Speaking extra

## Getting more information

**1** ★ ▶ **7.3** **Join the parts of the sentences.**

1 If I'd just gone to bed at a normal time,
2 I wasn't sure about joining at all,
3 They invited me, but I had to do a week of summer school –
4 I had the application filled out and everything,
5 If she gave me another chance,
6 Most of the mistakes I've made,

a I would apologise right away.
b it ended up being the best vacation ever, and I missed it.
c but my parents said I should.
d I've learned from. So are they really mistakes?
e I would have done a lot better.
f but then, at the last minute, I got nervous and didn't send it.

**2** ★ 🔊 **27** **Listen to the conversation. Where was Omar's dad's mobile phone?**

**3** ★★ 🔊 **27** **Complete the conversation with the words in the box. Then listen again and check.**

| know | that | lucky | anything | then |

**Ellen:** Oh, what's this … Is this a new phone?
**Omar:** You've found it! I've been looking for that all afternoon. If I'd lost it, I'd have been in big trouble. My dad's lent it to me.
**Ellen:** Really – why is ¹_____ ?
**Omar:** Well, he's let me borrow it so that I can call him after the concert tonight. But, you'll never guess what I did earlier …
**Ellen:** What?
**Omar:** I dropped it down the stairs!
**Ellen:** No! Does your dad ²_____ ?
**Omar:** Yes, he does. He was there! In fact, it hit him on the head.
**Ellen:** Did he say ³_____ ?
**Omar:** Of course. He was really angry.
**Ellen:** Oh no! So ⁴_____ what happened?
**Omar:** Well … I switched it on and it still worked.
**Ellen:** That was ⁵_____ !
**Omar:** So, Dad told me to put it in a safe place, and I did, but I forgot where I'd put it! It must have slipped down the side of the sofa.
**Ellen:** Why didn't you just call it?
**Omar:** Oh, yeah. That's a good idea! Why didn't I think of that?

## Pronunciation focus

**4** ★ 🔊 **28** **Listen to the sentences. Which words or parts of words are stressed in each one? Listen and repeat.**

1 Really – why was that?
2 That was lucky!
3 Did your mum know?
4 Oh no! So then what happened?
5 Did she say anything?

**5** ★ 🔊 **29** **Listen to the conversation. What happened to Ruby's trainers?**

**6** ★★★ 🔊 **29** **Listen again and complete the conversation.**

**Lucy:** Wow! I love those trainers.
**Ruby:** Oh, thanks. I only bought them last week. But they almost got me into a lot of trouble.
**Lucy:** Really – ¹_____ ?
**Ruby:** Well, the first day I put them on, right, I was running and I fell and there was a big black mark across the left shoe! The first day … !
**Lucy:** Oh no! So ²_____ ?
**Ruby:** Well, when I got home, I went into the kitchen and started to clean them. And then my mum walked in.
**Lucy:** Did ³_____ ?
**Ruby:** Yes, she said 'I'm glad to see you're looking after those new trainers'!!!
**Lucy:** So ⁴_____ not know?
**Ruby:** No, she didn't!! She thought I was just cleaning them.
**Lucy:** And where's the big black mark?
**Ruby:** Oh, I cleaned it off … it was actually very easy.
**Lucy:** Wow! ⁵_____ !

**7** ★★ 🔊 **29** **Listen again and check your answers. Then listen and repeat the conversation.**

# Speaking extra

## Clarifying

**1** ★ ▶ 8.3 **Join the parts of the sentences.**

1 A classmate once told me that there was
2 My old best friend said she couldn't
3 My brother gave me a small, funny-looking tomato and told me
4 People kept saying
5 My grandma always used to tell me that
6 A boy in my class told everyone that

a if you eat carrots, you'll be able to see in the dark.
b it was really delicious.
c how cute I looked, which made it even worse.
d no school the next day.
e his cousin was Robert Pattinson.
f come shopping with me.

**2** ★ 🔊 30 **Listen to the conversation. Why is Stella interviewing Jeff?**

**3** ★★ 🔊 30 **Complete the conversation with the words in the box. Then listen again and check.**

> totally  right  absolutely  true
> comment  joking  false

**Stella:** So, thanks for the interview for your old school magazine, Jeff.
**Jeff:** It's my pleasure.
**Stella:** So we've heard that you're going to leave the band. Is that ¹_____?
**Jeff:** Look, these rumours are completely ²_____. I love being with the band. We've been on tour for the last year, travelling all around the world, and we're all really tired, so we're on a break.
**Stella:** Yes, but people are saying that you don't get on well with Andy, the singer. Would you like to ³_____ on that?
**Jeff:** Sure. Look all these stories about us not getting on … they're ⁴_____ untrue. I've known Andy since we were at the primary school just down the road from this school.
**Stella:** And is it ⁵_____ that you don't want Andy to come to your wedding?
**Jeff:** You must be ⁶_____! Andy is coming to my wedding – of course he is. He's my best friend!
**Stella:** OK, last question … are you really going to marry a girl you met at this school?
**Jeff:** Yes, ⁷_____. Daisy and I were at this school together for six years.

## Pronunciation focus

**4** ★ 🔊 31 **Listen to the sentences. Which word in each one has the strongest stress? Listen and repeat.**

1 These rumours are completely false.
2 They're totally untrue.
3 Yes, absolutely.
4 That is a really interesting story.

**5** ★ 🔊 32 **Listen to the conversation. What change would the head teacher make at the school?**

**6** ★★★ 🔊 32 **Listen again and complete the conversation.**

**Student:** So, Mr Jackman. Thank you for letting us interview you for the student website.
**Head teacher:** You're welcome.
**Student:** Now, we've heard that you sometimes sleep at the school in your office.
**Head teacher:** ¹_____! No, I go home every night, believe me.
**Student:** OK. There are some other rumours going around, too. ²_____ a TV station is coming to the school?
**Head teacher:** What? A TV station? Here? I'm afraid that rumour ³_____.
**Student:** Well, we heard that they're going to make a reality TV programme about life in the school. ⁴_____?
**Head teacher:** Well, I think it would be a great idea. But no, ⁵_____, sorry.
**Student:** And, ⁶_____ on the rumour that you want to introduce a school uniform next year?
**Head teacher:** ⁷_____! That is true. It would make everyone's life so much easier if they wore the same clothes.

**7** ★★ 🔊 32 **Listen again and check your answers. Then listen and repeat the conversation.**

# Language focus extra

## Past simple vs. past continuous

**1** Complete the sentences with the past simple or past continuous form of the verbs in brackets.

1 Mathew ___was playing___ (play) in the garden when he _____ (find) a gold coin.

2 Elena _____ (not hear) the teacher's question because she _____ (chat).

3 While we _____ (fish) last weekend, we _____ (catch) a large fish.

4 Lisa _____ (not see) the end of the film because she _____ (talk) on her phone.

5 They _____ (not go) out yesterday because it _____ (rain) all day.

## Present perfect and past simple

**2** Complete the email with the present perfect or past simple form of the verbs in brackets.

Hi Ollie,

How [1]___were___ (be) your holidays? We [2]_____ (go) to Portugal for two weeks. We [3]_____ (cycle) along the coast and [4]_____ (eat) lots of delicious food! Term [5]_____ (begin) last Monday and I [6]_____ (start) at my new school. I [7]_____ (not be) here very long, but I love it! I [8]_____ (make) some new friends and I [9]_____ (join) the football team. I [10]_____ (not have) any homework back, but I hope they aren't too strict!

Your friend,

Lucy

## Present perfect with still, yet, already and just

**3** Circle the correct words.

A: Nick, have you finished your project [1]still / yet?
B: Yes, I've [2]just / yet finished!

C: I wrote to Mike this morning but he [3]still / already hasn't replied.
D: Well, maybe he hasn't checked his email [4]yet / already.

E: Have you eaten dinner [5]still / yet?
F: Yes. We eat early in our house – we've [6]already / yet finished!

## Word order in questions

**4** Circle the correct options.

1 You do / Do you go to school by bus?
2 What is he / he is doing tonight?
3 Were they / They were at home last night?
4 How long did you / you did live in France?
5 Are you / You are from Italy?

## Subject/object questions

**5** Write questions for these answers.

1 Who ____won first prize____ ?
Sally won first prize.

2 Who _____ ?
Rob sings the best.

3 What _____ ?
They watched a football match.

4 Who _____ ?
Their dad watched them play.

5 What _____ ?
Music makes me happy.

## Present perfect with ever, never, for and since

**6** Complete the mini-conversations.

A: Have you [1]___ever___ been to Australia?
B: No, but I've wanted to go [2]_____ I was a child.
A: Really? My aunt has lived there [3]_____ ten years – she loves it.

C: Have you [4]_____ played the violin?
D: Yes, I've had violin lessons [5]_____ I was ten.
C: Really! I've [6]_____ heard you play!

## Present perfect questions

**7** Write questions with the present perfect.

1 he / buy / the concert tickets / yet?
*Has he bought the concert tickets yet?*

2 How long / he / live / in London?
_____

3 they / take / their test / yet?
_____

4 you / ever / go / Hawaii?
_____

5 Where / she / go / for her holiday?
_____

# Language focus extra

## used to and would

**1** **Rewrite the underlined phrases using *used to* or *would*. If both are possible, use *would*. If neither is possible, write X.**

1 We <u>went</u> to the cinema every afternoon when I was young.
*would go*_____

2 <u>Did you have</u> long hair when you were young?
_____

3 I <u>saw</u> the Rolling Stones once in Hyde Park.
_____

4 Where <u>did you live</u> when you were at college?
_____

5 We <u>didn't have</u> a lot of money in those days.
_____

6 They <u>sat</u> in coffee shops all day when they were students.
_____

7 She <u>didn't eat</u> meat even when she was a child.
_____

8 <u>Did you go</u> to the Isle of Wight Festival in 1980?
_____

**2** **Complete the conversation with the correct form of *used to* or *would*. If both are possible, use *would*.**

**Julie:** What kind of music ¹____*did*____ you ____*use to*____ like when you were younger?

**Dad:** Oh we ²_____ listen to all kinds of music. Your mother and I ³_____ like soul and reggae.

**Julie:** Really? ⁴_____ you _____ go to concerts together?

**Dad:** Oh yes, all the time! We ⁵_____ hang out with the musicians after the concerts and we ⁶_____ get home until 3 or 4 o'clock in the morning.

**Julie:** That sounds cool! How ⁷_____ you _____ get home?

**Dad:** We ⁸_____ have a car, so we ⁹_____ walk all the way home hand in hand under the stars and we ¹⁰_____ sing all our favourite songs.

**Julie:** That sounds romantic!

## Past perfect

**3** **Complete the sentences with the correct form of the verbs in brackets. Use the past simple and the past perfect in each sentence.**

1 Karen _____*went*_____ (go) home because she ____*had forgotten*____ (forget) her ticket.

2 _____ you _____ (hear) of this band before we _____ (see) them last week?

3 We _____ (be) late for school because we _____ (miss) the early bus.

4 Hayley _____ (be) upset because they _____ (not invite) her to their party.

5 I only _____ (pass) my driving test after I _____ (take) it three times.

6 Sam _____ (play) with three different bands before he _____ (become) famous.

7 How many stories _____ you _____ (write) before you _____ (publish) your first book?

8 We _____ (go) to the Thai restaurant because _____ (not try) Thai food before.

9 _____ they _____ (climb) any mountains before they _____ (go) to Kilimanjaro?

10 How long _____ she _____ (live) in Japan before she _____ (meet) her boyfriend?

**4** **Complete the paragraph with the past simple or the past perfect form of the verbs in brackets.**

Have you seen this photo? It's my aunt at Glastonbury 1992. It was the first time she ¹_____*went*_____ (go) to a music festival. She ²_____ (never/go) to Glastonbury before but she ³_____ (always/want) to go and all her friends ⁴_____ (have) a crazy time there the year before. Anyway, when she ⁵_____ (get) there, the whole place ⁶_____ (be) packed. She ⁷_____ (never/see) so many tents before. Then she realised she ⁸_____ (not bring) her tent! Luckily, her friends ⁹_____ (arrive) the day before and they ¹⁰_____ (set) up a large tent and she ¹¹_____ (stay) there with them. They ¹²_____ (dance) to music all night long. It's strange – I can't imagine her at a festival, she's so serious nowadays!

# Language focus extra

## Reflexive pronouns and *each other*

**1 Complete the sentences with reflexive pronouns or *each other*.**

1 Maria introduced ____*herself*____ to her new classmates.

2 I often talk to _____ when I'm in the shower.

3 Can we help _____ to some more cake?

4 You need to prepare _____ for the test next week.

5 My brother hurt _____ when he was working in the garden.

6 My friends and I don't send _____ birthday cards anymore – we send emails.

7 This cooker turns _____ off when the clock rings.

8 My mum and dad really enjoyed _____ at our school concert.

9 My brother and I hadn't seen _____ for ages.

10 My sister taught _____ to play the saxophone.

**2 Circle the correct words.**

Dear Lisa,

I'm really enjoying ¹**myself** / me at my new dance class. Last week, we were very busy preparing ²**ourselves / us** for the end-of-term performance. All our parents came and watched ³**ourselves / us** in a new dance performance. I had a solo. I have a large mirror at home so that I can see ⁴**myself / me** while I'm practising. The performance was on Saturday. My best friend took a video of ⁵**itself / it**. I told ⁶**myself / me** not to be nervous, but it's really difficult to stay calm – how do professional dancers keep ⁷**themselves / them** calm? Do you think they have a special technique to help ⁸**themselves / them** not to be nervous? Anyway, I can send ⁹**yourself / you** some photos! Please write with your news. We haven't seen ¹⁰**each other / ourselves** for ages – let's meet soon!

Love, Carmen

## Present perfect simple

**3 Complete the mini-conversations with the present perfect form of the verbs in brackets.**

> **A:** How many slices of cake ¹____*have*____ you ____*eaten*____ (eat) today?
> **B:** I ²_____ (not have) many – only three slices including this one!

**C:** ³_____ you _____ (hear) of this film?

**D:** Of course! I think I ⁴_____ (see) it about five times. But I can watch it again, it's brilliant!

**E:** I ⁵_____ (play) this new computer game ten times. It's really popular!

**F:** Really? How many times ⁶_____ you _____ (win) so far?

**G:** Where's Suzie? I ⁷_____ (not see) her today.

**H:** I don't know. She ⁸_____ (be) absent for four days now.

**I:** ⁹_____ Jason _____ (finish) this book?

**J:** No, he ¹⁰_____ only _____ (read) three chapters.

## Present perfect continuous

**4 Complete the sentences with the present perfect continuous form of the verbs in the box.**

> go ~~have~~ play read call collect
> take visit walk study

1 How long ____*have*____ you ____*been having*____ guitar lessons? You're really good!

2 _____ Suzanna _____ Italian this year? Does she like it?

3 Jack and Harry _____ computer games in the library every Saturday.

4 Where _____ they _____ on Sunday afternoons? They're never home!

5 Why _____ you _____ to school every day? Don't you like the bus?

6 I _____ her on the phone all day but she doesn't answer!

7 _____ you _____ that new music blog? It's great!

8 We _____ photos of all the buildings in our town for our website.

9 Mel _____ the art museum every weekend to learn about art.

10 Our school _____ winter clothing for homeless people this winter.

# Language focus extra

## *be going to* and present tenses for the future

**1** **Match the sentences (1–10) with the correct descriptions (A–C).**

1 Martina is going to study medicine.
2 The summer holidays start next week!
3 We're going to play tennis every day.
4 I'm staying with my friend Gina this summer.
5 My art class finishes in September.
6 We're graduating in June.
7 I leave for Tokyo tomorrow morning.
8 They're going to have a party on Saturday.
9 We're going to a concert tomorrow.
10 I'm not going to come out tonight – I'm too tired.

**A** future intention      *1* __ __ __
**B** future arrangement    __ __ __
**C** scheduled future event   __ __ __

**2** **Circle the correct options.**

This summer I ¹**'m going** / **'ll go** on a tour of China with my family. We ²**'re visiting** / **visit** some friends of my parents who live in Beijing. First, we ³**'re staying** / **'re going to stay** with them for five days and after that we ⁴**'re taking** / **take** a bus tour to some ancient historic sites. Our flight ⁵**leaves** / **will leave** next Tuesday at 6 am (horribly early!) and it ⁶**arrives** / **is arriving** at 6 am the next day. I ⁷**'m going to learn** / **learn** some Chinese phrases before I go, and when I get back, I ⁸**'m going to apply** / **'m applying** for a Chinese language course – everyone says it's the language of the future, not English! The course ⁹**starts** / **'s starting** in September and it ¹⁰**takes** / **is taking** one year. I'm really looking forward to our trip and to learning a new language and about a new culture!

## Predictions with *be going to, will* and *may/might*

**3** **Complete the predictions with the correct form of the verbs in the boxes.**

> need ~~be~~ give become
> break lend pass miss

> might / ~~be going to~~

'I haven't brought a coat.' 'It's OK. It
¹ *isn't going to be* cold. They said so on the radio.'
'Is it cold outside?' 'Yes, I think you
²_____ a coat later on.'

> might / will

'I'm nervous about the exam.' 'Don't worry – I'm sure you ³_____ .'
'Can I carry those glasses for you?' 'Yes, but be careful – you ⁴_____ them.'

> be going to / might

'Oh no! It's already too late – we
⁵_____ the train!'
'Do you think Daniel ⁶_____ us a lift in his car?' 'I'm not sure. I'll ask him.'

> may / will

'I need to borrow some brown shoes.' 'Brooke has some. She ⁷_____ you hers.'
'Do you feel confident about the future?' 'Yes, totally. I ⁸_____ a millionaire before I'm 21!'

## Future continuous

**4** **Write future continuous questions about the year 2030 with the prompts.**

1 people / live / until they're 150?
*Will people be living until they're 150?*

2 How / we / spend / our free time?
_____

3 Where / people / go / on holiday?
_____

4 What fashions / we / wear?
_____

5 children / go / to school?
_____

6 What type of food / people / eat?
_____

**5** **Write answers to the questions in Exercise 4 using the future continuous.**

1 Yes / They / live / until they're 150
*Yes, they will. They'll be living until they're 150.*

2 People / not read / books anymore
_____

3 Spaceships / take / people to Mars for their holidays
_____

4 We / design / our own clothes on computers
_____

5 No / Children / do / all their classes online
_____

6 Restaurants / serve / seaweed instead of vegetables
_____

# Language focus extra

## First conditional with *if*, *when* and *unless*

**1** (Circle) the correct words.

1 I ('ll cook)/ cook an omelette if you (are)/ 'll be hungry.

2 If you **make / don't make** the toast, I **'ll cook / cook** the eggs.

3 The sauce will get thicker **unless / when** you **add / 'll add** the flour.

4 You won't get any dessert **unless / if** you **eat / 'll eat** all your vegetables.

5 I **'ll make / make** tea and coffee when the guests **arrive / will arrive**.

6 If we **eat / 'll eat** out tonight, I **won't / don't** have to cook dinner!

7 Mum **might make / makes** a chocolate cake for you **unless / if** you ask her nicely.

8 If you **'ll hurry / hurry** up, we **might get / get** to the fish and chip shop before it closes.

**2** Complete the conversations with the missing words. (Circle) the correct options.

**A**

**Clare:** Would you like to come over for dinner tonight? I ¹___ pizza if you ²___ the dessert. How does that sound?

**Rosie:** Great! ³___ I have time, I ⁴___ some ice cream from the supermarket on the way.

| | | | | | |
|---|---|---|---|---|---|
| 1 | **a** make | **b** 'm making | **c** 'll make |
| 2 | **a** brings | **b** bring | **c** 'll bring |
| 3 | **a** If | **b** When | **c** Unless |
| 4 | **a** 'll buy | **b** 'm buying | **c** buy |

**B**

**Chris:** Where do you want to sit? If we ¹___ a table by the window, we ²___ a great view.

**Martina:** Yes, but it ³___ not be so noisy if we ⁴___ here in the corner.

| | | | | | |
|---|---|---|---|---|---|
| 1 | **a** get | **b** gets | **c** 'll get |
| 2 | **a** have | **b** 'll have | **c** 're having |
| 3 | **a** might | **b** won't | **c** is |
| 4 | **a** 're sitting | **b** 'll sit | **c** sit |

**C**

**Joey:** If I ¹___ butter to this recipe, do you think it ²___ better?

**Mum:** Definitely! But remember that it won't cook ³___ you ⁴___ up the heat.

| | | | | | |
|---|---|---|---|---|---|
| 1 | **a** add | **b** 'll add | **c** 'm adding |
| 2 | **a** tastes | **b** 's tasting | **c** 'll taste |
| 3 | **a** if | **b** when | **c** unless |
| 4 | **a** 'll turn | **b** turns | **c** turn |

## Second conditional with *could* and *might*

**3** Write second conditional sentences with the prompts.

1 If / Suzanna / have / enough money / go / to expensive restaurants

If *Suzanna had enough money, she'd go to expensive restaurants* .

2 Martin / could go / cycling in the park / not have / so much homework

Martin _____ .

3 If / we / not be / so busy / might go / to the beach this weekend

If _____ .

4 Sam and Christy / not ask / for help / unless / they / really need / it

Sam and Christy _____ .

5 If / someone / give / me / a free ticket to any country / I / go / to Australia

If _____ .

6 I / not eat / raw fish / unless / be / in a Japanese restaurant

I _____ .

**4** Write questions for these answers.

1 What *would you do if you didn't need to study this weekend* ?

If I didn't need to study this weekend, I might go shopping, or I might watch a movie.

2 How _____ ?

If we shared a bedroom, we'd argue every day.

3 How _____ ?

If he didn't talk to me, I'd feel very sad.

4 What _____ ?

If I could have any superpower, I'd like to be able to fly.

5 Where _____ ?

If I could fly, I'd go to the moon.

6 Who _____ ?

If I could meet any film star, I'd choose Johnny Depp.

# Language focus extra

## The passive: present simple, past simple and *will*

**1** **Complete the sentences with the correct active or passive form of the verbs in brackets.**

1  The first email _____ *was sent* _____ (send) by Ray Tomlinson in 1971.

2  In 1990, Tim Berners-Lee _____ (develop) the World Wide Web.

3  Today, emails _____ (send) by millions of people all over the world.

4  The first radio waves _____ (transmit) by Marconi in 1895.

5  _____ radio waves _____ (use) to communicate with other planets in the future?

6  Louis Daguerre _____ (take) the first photograph in 1839.

7  Photographs are still popular, but film _____ (not use) anymore.

8  Penicillin _____ (discover) by Alexander Fleming in 1928.

9  How many illnesses _____ (prevent) by using penicillin nowadays?

10  In future, many diseases _____ (treat) using DNA or gene therapy.

**2** **Rewrite the text using the passive. Add *by* if necessary.**

The invention of paper money

[1] The Chinese invented paper money in the 9th century AD. [2] Merchants signed certificates promising to pay a certain amount of money. [3] They called the paper money 'flying money' because it flew away so easily. [4] European countries did not introduce paper money until more than 500 years later. [5] A Swedish bank printed the first bank note in 1661. [6] Today, people use bank notes all over the world. [7] People also make many payments using digital systems. [8] In the future, digital money will replace physical money. [9] People won't use coins or notes anymore. [10] You'll only find them in museums and in history books.

1  *Paper money was invented by the Chinese in the 9th century AD.*

2  _____

3  _____

4  _____

5  _____

6  _____

7  _____

8  _____

9  _____

10  _____

## Relative pronouns and clauses

**3** **Circle the correct words.**

A new kind of robot

Computer scientists [1]**which / who** have invented a new type of robot have just won a prize for technological innovation. They've invented a robot [2]**that / where** can walk and run just like a human. People [3]**where / whose** jobs involve working in places [4]**where / which** are dangerous for humans will find many uses for this type of robot. The robots can also work in homes [5]**where / which** the disabled or the elderly need many types of routine care. Many tasks [6]**which / whose** elderly people find difficult could eventually be done by robots. Other places [7]**which / where** robots may become common include supermarkets, hospitals and schools. But some people are afraid that in the future robots [8]**that / whose** intelligence is superior to humans may take over the planet.

**4** **Complete the text using the relative clauses below.**

A new way to communicate

An amazing invention [1]*a* at the Google Science Fair recently was a communication device called TALK. It was invented by a 16-year-old boy from India [2]___ . His invention is a device [3]___ into letters. It is much cheaper than other systems [4]___ – some of them can cost over $5,000. People [5]___ need to wear a special sensor. The sensor is placed [6]___ variations in the person's breath, generally under the nose. People [7]___ make it difficult for them to speak can use this device to communicate. Arsh has a website [8]___ about his invention and his plans for research.

a  ~~that won an award~~

b  where it can detect

c  where you can read

d  which changes human breath

e  which are currently available

f  whose name is Arsh Dilbagi

g  who use the device

h  whose medical conditions

# Language focus extra

## -ing forms

**1** Complete the text with the *-ing* form of the verbs in the box.

> chat  dance  buy  dress  stand  try  walk
> go (x2)  say  look  help  worry  make

I love ¹___*going*___ to parties. I like ²_____ up and I enjoy ³_____ to music, but I hate ⁴_____ with people that I don't know. ⁵_____ new friends is really hard! My mum says I need to practise ⁶_____ to be more confident. What can I do?

My sister's having her engagement party this weekend. I don't mind ⁷_____ to plan the party, but she wants me to make a speech! I can't imagine myself ⁸_____ up in front of all those people! I'm terrified of ⁹_____ stupid! ¹⁰_____ about it is keeping me awake at night. What should I do?

My mum is crazy about ¹¹_____ shopping at the weekends, but ¹²_____ clothes is my least favourite activity! ¹³_____ around big department stores is so boring! I don't want to upset her by ¹⁴_____ I don't want to go. What can I do?

## Infinitives

**2** Write sentences with the prompts. Use the past simple of the verbs provided and infinitives where necessary.

1  My sister / offer / lend / me / her new handbag
   *My sister offered to lend me her new handbag.*

2  Simon / invite / me / dance / with him
   _____

3  We / be / amazed / get / free concert tickets
   _____

4  We / agree / watch / the fireworks / tonight
   _____

5  My friend / ask / us / go / to a party
   _____

6  It / be / difficult / talk / because of the noise
   _____

7  We / be / ready / leave / ten minutes ago
   _____

8  Which dress / you / decide / wear?
   _____

## Infinitives vs. -ing forms

**3** Circle the infinitives and *-ing* forms in these sentences and look at the words before them. Then match them to the rules.

1  I was amazed (to see) so many people at the play.
2  They suggested decorating the room with flowers.
3  Sally's parents offered to take us to the prom.
4  I imagine people listening to my music on stage.
5  Playing computer games is a total waste of time!
6  He taught her to play the guitar.
7  I'm excited about playing in the school concert.

a  We use the *-ing* form as a noun, and to make noun phrases. ___
b  We use the *-ing* form after certain verbs and certain expressions. ___
c  Some verbs can have an object before the *-ing* form. ___
d  We use the *-ing* form after prepositions. ___
e  We usually use the infinitive with *to* after adjectives. _1_
f  We use the infinitive with *to* after certain verbs. ___
g  Some verbs usually need an object before the infinitive with *to*. ___

**4** Circle the correct words.

**Debbi:** I want ¹(to celebrate) / celebrating the end of our course – let's have a costume party!
**Dave:** Are you joking? I can't stand ²to dress / dressing up.
**Debbi:** I think people will enjoy ³to design / designing their own costumes – it'll be fun!
**Dave:** I suppose so … but I'm hopeless at ⁴to plan / planning parties.
**Debbi:** Don't worry. I'm brilliant at ⁵to organise / organising things! ⁶To find / Finding a place to have the party is no problem. My dad agreed ⁷to lend / lending us the garage for a party last year, so I'll ask him again.
**Dave:** OK, so what can I do?
**Debbi:** I'd like you ⁸to get / getting hold of some lights and something to play music.
**Dave:** OK. That's easy ⁹to do / doing. How many people do you plan ¹⁰to invite / inviting?
**Debbi:** Everyone in our class!
**Dave:** That's thirty people – I recommend ¹¹to ask / asking your neighbours if they mind us ¹²to have / having a party in your garage – it could get very noisy!

# Language focus extra

## Third conditional

**1** **Write third conditional sentences with the prompts. Use the words in brackets.**

1 Why didn't you set the alarm? (not be late)
If *you had set the alarm, you wouldn't have been late* .

2 Why did he step off the path? (not fall into the lake)
He _____
_____ .

3 Why did she leave her phone in the car? (call the police)
If _____
_____ .

4 Why didn't we bring any money? (buy some food)
We _____
_____ .

5 Why did you make so much noise? (not wake the neighbours)
If _____
_____ .

6 Why wasn't he more careful? (not break the window)
He _____
_____ .

**2** **Complete the third conditional sentences with the correct form of the verbs in brackets.**

1 If we ___*hadn't climbed*___ (not climb) the mountain, we ___*wouldn't have seen*___ (not see) the giant footprints.

2 No one _____ (believe) us if we _____ (not take) a photo.

3 If you _____ (not wake) me up, I _____ (not see) the shooting stars.

4 Vicky _____ (not lose) her way, if the sign _____ (be) clearer.

5 They _____ (not find) him in the snow if he _____ (not have) his phone.

6 What _____ (you/do) if you _____ (see) an alien spaceship?

7 _____ (you/go) into the cave if you _____ (hear) a strange noise?

8 How _____ (he/escape) if they _____ (not follow) him?

## *must have, can't have, might/may/could have*

**3** **Write sentences with *must have, can't have* and *might/may/could have*. Use the ideas in brackets.**

1 Maria didn't go to school last week. (Maybe she was ill.)
She *might have been ill* .

2 Michael got a zero in his test. (I'm sure he didn't study much.)
He _____ .

3 They were late. (Maybe they missed the bus.)
They _____ .

4 He got a new bike. (I'm sure it was his birthday.)
It _____ .

5 The film doesn't come out until Friday. (I'm sure you haven't seen it yet.)
You _____ .

6 There was a lot of loud music next door last night. (I'm sure they had a party.)
They _____ .

**4** **Complete the mini-conversations. Use *must have, can't have* and *might/may/could have* and the correct form of the verbs in the box.**

> ~~go~~   decide   go   leave   feel   take   put   go

A: Where's Lucas? Has he gone home already?
B: No, he [1] ___*can't have gone*___ home because his bag is still here on his chair.
A: Yes … he [2] _____ for a coffee. Or maybe he's outside.

C: Oh no! I can't find my keys!
D: Do you think you [3] _____ them in your coat pocket?
C: I don't think so … Oh I know!
I [4] _____ them in the door again!

E: Do you think the neighbours have gone on holiday?
F: No, they [5] _____ on holiday – look their car's parked outside.
E: Yes, but [6] _____ they _____ a taxi to the airport?

G: Isn't Gina coming to the film with us?
H: I think she [7] _____ to stay at home. She was feeling tired. I'll text her to check.
G: Well … I'm sure she [8] _____ exhausted when she finished her exam earlier, but maybe she feels better now.

# Language focus extra

## Reported statements

**1 Complete the police officer's report.**

*The police received a mysterious phone message:*
'Hello. My name is Mike. I live on Greenwood Road. I saw some strange men going into the house next door. They looked very suspicious. I haven't seen them here before. I don't want to cause any trouble, but I think they might be spies. I can't remember anything else. I'll call you if I see them again.'

*The police officer reported the message to the chief inspector:*
'Good morning, chief. This morning we received a message from a man. He told us that his name ¹_____*was*_____ Mike and that he
²_____ on Greenwood Road. He said he ³_____ some strange men going into the house next door. He said they
⁴_____ very suspicious and that he
⁵_____ them there before. He told us that he ⁶_____ to cause any trouble, but he ⁷_____ they might be spies. He said that he ⁸_____ anything else but he ⁹_____ us if he ¹⁰_____ them again.'

**2 Complete the reported statements. Remember to change pronouns and time references.**

1  Martin: 'Shelley was here yesterday.'
   Martin said that Shelley *had been there the day before* .

2  Jake: 'I saw this film a week ago.'
   Jake told me _____
   _____ .

3  Vicky: 'I'm not sure what time I'll finish work this evening.'
   Vicky told me _____
   _____ .

4  Sam: 'We haven't seen the film yet, but the reviews were very good.'
   Sam told me that they _____
   _____ .

5  Jasmin: 'Keira will call you tomorrow.'
   Jasmin said that Keira _____
   _____ .

6  Ellen: 'Maria can't come to the concert.'
   Ellen said that Maria _____
   _____ .

## Reported questions

**3 Read the police interview. Then complete the text with reported questions.**

| | |
|---|---|
| **Officer:** | Can you answer some questions, please? |
| **Emma:** | Yes, of course. What is it about? |
| **Officer:** | Where were you this morning at 10 am? |
| **Emma:** | I was at home all day. |
| **Officer:** | Did you hear any unusual noises? |
| **Emma:** | No, I didn't. What's happened? |
| **Officer:** | It's just routine. |
| **Emma:** | Has there been a crime? |
| **Officer:** | We're investigating a robbery. |
| **Emma:** | Where did the robbery take place? |
| **Officer:** | It was next door to you. Have you spoken to any neighbours today? |
| **Emma:** | No, I haven't. |
| **Officer:** | Please will you get in touch if you hear any information? |

The officer asked me
¹*if I could answer some questions* . She asked me ²_____ .
I said I'd been at home all day. She asked me
³_____ . I said no. Then
I asked her ⁴_____ .
She said it was routine. I asked her
⁵_____ and she said they were investigating a robbery. I asked her
⁶_____ . And she said it had been next door to my house! She asked me
⁷_____ . And then she asked me ⁸_____ .

## Indirect questions

**4 Rewrite the direct questions as indirect questions.**

1  Where do you live?
   Could you tell us *where you live?* _____

2  What is your address?
   Could I ask _____

3  What did you see?
   Could you tell me _____

4  Who called the police?
   Do you know _____

5  Did you see the car number plate?
   I was wondering _____

6  Did you notice their appearance?
   Can I ask _____

7  Where do you work?
   Can you tell us _____

8  Could you come with us to the police station?
   We were wondering _____

# Thanks and acknowledgments

The authors and publishers would like to thank a number of people whose support has proved invaluable during the planning, writing and production process of this course.

We would like to thank Diane Nicholls for researching and writing the Get it right! pages and Ingrid Wisniewska for writing the Grammar extra section.

We would like to thank Tim Foster for bringing his warmth and experience to the project and for his reliable and keen-eyed editorial work.

We would also like to thank the teams of educational consultants, representatives and managers working for Cambridge University Press in various countries around the world.

The authors and publishers are grateful to the following contributors:

Blooberry: concept design
emc design limited: text design and layouts
QBS Learning: photo selection and cover design
DSound, Soundtracks Studios & Ian Harker: audio production

Development of this publication has made use of the Cambridge English Corpus (CEC). The CEC is a computer database of contemporary spoken and written English, which currently stands at over one billion words. It includes British English, American English and other varieties of English. It also includes the Cambridge Learner Corpus, developed in collaboration with the University of Cambridge ESOL Examinations. Cambridge University Press has built up the CEC to provide evidence about language use that helps to produce better language teaching materials.

The authors and publishers acknowledge the following sources of copyright material and are grateful for the permissions granted. While every effort has been made, it has not always been possible to identify the sources of all the material used, or to trace all copyright holders. If any omissions are brought to our notice, we will be happy to include the appropriate acknowledgements on reprinting.

p. 3 (CL): Getty Images/Heath Korvola; p. 3 (BR): Getty Images/Saša Prudkov; p. 4 (CR): Alamy/©Jan Wlodarczyk; p. 5 (BR): Getty Images/ Hjalmeida; p. 8 (TR): Getty Images/Jay Blakesberg; p. 9 (TL): Getty Images/Wavebreak Media; p. 9 (BC): Getty Images/Peet Simard; p. 9 (BR): Alamy/©Kuttig - Travel; p. 10 (BL): Alamy/©Picture Partners; p. 11 (BL): Alamy/©Jamie Pham Photography; p. 12: Getty Images/ Michael Ochs Archives/Stringer; p. 15 (BR): Shutterstock Images/ Syda Productions; p. 17 (CR): Alamy/©Richard Levine; p. 19 (B): Alamy/©HelloWorld Images Premium; p. 20 (CR): Shutterstock Images/Joggie Botma; p. 21 (BL): Alamy/©Allan Zilkowsky; p. 22 (TR): Alamy/©Nico Smit; p. 27 (BL): Alamy/©National Geographic Image Collection; p. 28 (BL): Alamy/©Image Source; p. 29 (TL): Shutterstock Images/arek_malang; p. 29 (TR): Getty Images/Buda Mendes; p. 29 (CR): Getty Images/Udit Kulshrestha/Bloomberg; p. 29 (BR): Alamy/©Everett Collection Inc; p. 30 (CR): Getty Images/ John Lamparski/WireImage; p. 30 (B/G): Shutterstock Images/Philip Birtwistle; p. 31 (T): Alamy/©Natalia Kuzmina; p. 31 (C): Shutterstock Images/Morrowind; p. 31 (B): Shutterstock Images/Bohbeh; p. 32 (CR): Getty Images/Bart Coenders; p. 35 (CR): REX/ITV; p. 37 (1): Shutterstock Images/Angelika Smile; p. 37 (2): Shutterstock Images/ Ron Vargas; p. 37 (3): Getty Images/Clubfoto; p. 37 (4): Getty Images/ Michael Powell; p. 37 (5): Getty Images/Daniel Loiselle; p. 37 (6): Getty Images/Ac_bnphotos; p. 37 (7): Alamy/©Ajcgoldberg/Stockimo; p. 37 (8): Shutterstock Images/NinaM; p. 37 (9): Alamy/©SoFood; p. 37 (10): Shutterstock Images/M. Unal Ozmen; p. 37 (TR): Alamy/©Jonathan Goldberg; p. 37 (CR): Shutterstock Images/Mariontxa; p. 37 (BR): Corbis/The food passionates; p. 38 (BL): Shutterstock Images/CandyBox Images; p. 38 (BC): Alamy/©a-plus image bank; p. 38 (TR): Getty Images/William Shaw; p. 38 (TC): Shutterstock Images/Foxy's Forest Manufacture; p. 38 (CR): Shutterstock Images/Roman Sigaev; p. 39 (1): Shutterstock Images/pavelgr; p. 39 (2): Shutterstock Images/dinsor; p. 39 (3): Getty Images/Doable/A.collection; p. 39 (4): Getty Images/ Juanmonino; p. 39 (5): Shutterstock Images/Africa Studio; p. 39 (6): Alamy/©Radius Images; p. 39 (7): Getty Images/GooDween123; p. 39 (8): Getty Images/Paul Poplis; p. 39 (9): Shutterstock Images/ Dulce Rubia; p. 39 (10): Alamy/©Mediablitzimages; p. 39 (CR): Getty Images/Jon Feingersh; p. 40 (CR): Alamy/©MBI; p. 41 (TL): Alamy/©Art Directors & TRIP; p. 42 (TL): Shutterstock Images/Martin Turzak; p. 47 (BL): Alamy/©Frances Roberts; p. 48 (CL): Shutterstock Images/David Pruter; p. 48 (C): Alamy/©Judith Collins; p. 49 (TL): Shutterstock Images/GoBOb; p. 49 (CR): Alamy/©Olivier Parent; p. 50 (CL): Getty Images/Peopleimages; p. 51 (T): Getty Images/Clark_fang; p. 51 (C): Shutterstock Images/Prapann; p. 51 (B): Alamy/©keith van-Loen; p. 54 (TC): Alamy/©ACE STOCK LIMITED; p. 54 (CR): Alamy/©Zoonar GmbH; p. 55: Shutterstock Images/Joe Seer; p. 57 (CR): Corbis/BEAWIHARTA/ Reuters; p. 59 (T): Alamy/©Suzanne Long; p. 59 (BL): Getty Images/ Scott Campbell/Contributor; p. 60 (BL): Getty Images/Henglein and Steets; p. 61 (1): Corbis/Ricardo Azoury; p. 61 (2): Getty Images/Jeff J Mitchell; p. 61 (3): Getty Images/Buda Mendes/LatinContent; p. 61 (4): Getty Images/Anna Bryukhanova; p. 61 (5): Getty Images/Jeff J Mitchell; p. 61 (6): Alamy/©Richard Levine; p. 62 (TR): Alamy/©Image Broker; p. 64 (TR): Alamy/©Tetra Images; p. 65 (BL): Alamy/©J.R. Bale; p. 67 (CR): Rex Features/Â©20thCentFox/Courtesy Everett C; p. 68 (TR): Getty Images/Larry Williams/LWA/Blend Images; p. 69 (TL): Shutterstock Images/Vadim Petrakov; p. 69 (CR): Getty Images/Alfred Eisenstaedt/Pix./The LIFE Picture Collection; p. 70 (TR): Getty Images/ Harald Sund; p. 71 (T): Alamy/©Peter Polak; p. 71 (B): Shutterstock Images/Wavebreakmedia; p. 72 (T): Getty Images/David McNew; p. 74 (BL): Shutterstock Images/Vaclav Volrab; p. 75 (CL): Newscom/ Aeromobil/SIPA; p. 77 (A): Alamy/©Kenny Williamson Glasgow; p. 77 (B): Alamy/©Peter Titmuss; p. 79 (TR): Alamy/©Steve Skjold; p. 81 (TL): Alamy/©Stockex; p. 81 (TR): Alamy/©Steve Mansfield-Devine; p. 82 (BL): Alamy/©Louise Heusinkveld; p. 87: Getty Images/Lisa Stirling; p. 88: Alamy/©Pere Sanz; p. 89: Alamy/©Ian Shaw; p. 90: Alamy/©Amana images inc.; p. 91: Alamy/©British Retail Photography; p. 92: Alamy/©IanDagnall Computing; p. 93: Getty Images/Rainer Elstermann; p. 94: Alamy/©JeffreyIsaacGreenberg.

Front cover photograph by Getty Images/Eduardo Garcia.

The publishers are grateful to the following illustrators:

Anni Betts p. 7; Q2A Media Services, Inc. p. 6, 11, 14, 21, 27, 41, 51, 52, 78, 79, 80.